Gas Grill Cookouts

Simple to Sensational

It's no wonder gas grill cookouts have become such a popular custom. Today's gas grills are designed to give you the very best in outdoor cooking convenience. With your gas grill, you can prepare taste-tempting dishes out-of-doors with the same ease you've come to appreciate from your modern indoor cooking appliances.

If you aren't using your gas grill to cook more than hamburgers, hot dogs or an occasional steak, you're missing many of its benefits. This cookbook is designed to show you how to turn your gas grill into one of the most versatile, exciting cooking appliances you've ever owned. It contains step-by-step recipes, instructions and photographs to show you how to prepare complete menus for all occasions, from appetizers to desserts, from the simple to the sensational!

Gas Grill Cookouts — Simple To Sensational was created in response to your many requests for tips and techniques to help you develop your gas grill skills and utilize your gas grill to the fullest. A special thanks goes to Irma Broyles and Dale Bard of Preway Industries Inc. who served as consultants on this project. We also extend our sincerest appreciation to Cy DeCosse Incorporated who spent many long hours developing and writing what we believe is the finest gas grill cookbook available today.

Preway Industries Inc.

❶ This symbol indicates a reduced-calorie recipe.

Contents

Grilling Basics

Getting Ready

Outdoor grilling is one of to-day's most popular ways to cook. Juicy grilled burgers, crispy barbecued chicken and succulent roasts are just a few of the dishes that have made grilling such a favorite. *Grilling with gas makes outdoor cook-ing easier than ever.* You don't need to bother with charcoal or lighter fluid. And there's no long wait while the coals heat. Cooking on your covered gas grill also lets you enjoy the fun and flavor of grilling all year around. Rain, snow or cold can't stop you from grilling up a storm! *Clean-up is easy be-cause the mess stays out of your kitchen and there's no charcoal to dispose of.* Since

you're cooking outdoors, your kitchen stays cool on hot days.

With all these benefits, why restrict gas grilling to just ham-burgers and steaks? *Try an en-tire meal — everything from the appetizer to the dessert can be prepared on a gas grill.* Unlike charcoal grilling, gas grilling creates a smoky flavor only when meat juices fall on the lava rocks. Other foods will cook as they might on a range-top or in a conventional oven. Breads and desserts turn out moist and delicious. And vege-tables cook to perfection. Breakfast favorites are easy and tasty. *In this book, we've included recipes for all sorts*

of unique, delectable dishes that you never knew were possible on the grill! You'll also find new twists on everyday favorites like hamburgers, chicken and other basics.

In addition to many delectable recipes, we've included special guidelines and techniques to make your grilling easy and enjoyable. Everyone in the family will want to join in the fun. You'll learn to use your gas grill for all kinds of occasions — from easy everyday meals to elegant entertaining menus. *The convenience and delicious results of gas grilling make this an appliance you'll want to use for three meals a day!*

Before You Start

There are several factors to consider before you begin grilling: the weather conditions, the size of your grill and your individual tastes.

The outdoor temperature and amount of wind at the grilling site may cause cooking times to vary. On cold, windy days the heat setting specified in a recipe may be too low. Turn the control knob to a higher setting to compensate for the cold weather. The opposite occurs on warm, windless days. The suggested setting may be too hot and the control knob may need to be adjusted.

The size and BTU rating of your grill may also affect cooking times. The recipes in this book were formulated on 30,000 to 40,000 BTU grills. Grills with lower BTU ratings are smaller, so they may cook faster. If your grill has a lower rating, the cooking times in this book may need to be shortened.

Don't forget to consider your individual tastes for doneness when you grill. The cooking times we specify for rare meat may be too long if you like your meat *very* rare; adjust times accordingly. *Foods cooked on a gas grill tend to cook faster than foods cooked on other types of outdoor grills.* Watch food closely each time you grill until you are well acquainted with how your grill cooks.

Gas. Your grill operates on LP gas from a portable tank or natural gas from an underground gas line. If you're using gas from a tank, be sure it has enough gas before you grill. If your grill or tank is not equipped with a gas gauge, keep a spare tank handy so you won't run out while grilling. You don't need to bother with extra gas if your grill uses natural gas from an underground line.

Grid. To prevent food from sticking, season the cooking grid with butter, margarine, vegetable oil or vegetable cooking spray *before preheating the grill.*

Lava rocks. Before you light the grill, spread the rocks in an even layer on the lava rock grate. This helps spread the heat evenly under the cooking grid. When you ignite the burner, gas flames heat the lava rocks which in turn become hot and cook the food.

Lighting the grill. *Always open the hood before you light the burner* so gas doesn't become trapped inside the grill. Follow the instructions for lighting the burner in your grill use and care manual. Allow the lava rocks to heat before you start to cook. Close the hood and keep the heat setting at HIGH. To cook foods which require the HIGH or MEDIUM heat setting, preheat the grill for 6 to 10 minutes. For foods that cook at a lower temperature, preheat for only 2 to 5 minutes. Turn the control knob to the lower cooking temperature before adding the food.

Utensils & Accessories

The right equipment helps to make grilling safe, easy and enjoyable. Keep utensils and accessories in a convenient place so they're handy for all your grilling needs.

1. Wire brush. Use a stiff wire brush to clean the cooking grid after grilling. A brush with brass wire bristles and a long handle works best.

2. Long-handled utensils. Cooking utensils should have long handles that are heat resistant. Tongs, spatula and fork are handy for rearranging and turning food. A basting brush is ideal for brushing sauces, bastes and butters on meats and vegetables.

3. Oven mitt. Use oven mitts to protect your hands from heat and hot spatters from the grill.

4. Drip pan. When you smoke cook meats or cook on the rotisserie, place an aluminum or disposable foil drip pan on the lava rocks under the meat. This catches meat juices which otherwise fall onto the hot lava rocks and create flare-ups.

5. Grill-safe custard cups. These small bowls are useful for mixing sauces, bastes and butters. Place the cup on the edge of the cooking grid or upper cooking rack to keep the mixture warm and handy for brushing on foods.

6. Flat grill basket. Use this basket to grill foods like fish, ribs and chops. Place the basket directly on the cooking grid or attach it to the rotisserie spit.

7. Shelf with cutting board. Mount this handy shelf on the front of your grill to keep seasonings and grilling utensils within easy reach. The surface is also a convenient place to prepare meats and other foods for grilling.

8. Griddle. This utensil is ideal for preparing eggs, bacon, sausage or other grilled items. Fry up to four slices of bacon at a time. Drain the grease from the griddle surface before frying more.

9. Rotisserie. Use this popular accessory to slowly cook large cuts of meat or whole poultry. A motor-driven spit slowly rotates the food for even browning and cooking.

10. Pots and pans. Saucepans, Dutch ovens and large pots are useful for warming sauces and simmering stews. Pots and pans should be grill-safe, which means the entire pan and handle are ovenproof and flame-proof. Pans made of cast iron or glass ceramic (such as Corningware™) are ideal for cooking on the grill.

11. Casseroles and baking dishes. Many dishes you use in the conventional oven can be used to cook and bake in the gas grill. Dishes used directly on the lava rock grate must be grill-safe (ovenproof and flame-proof). Glass ceramic baking dishes such as Corningware™ are a good choice. *Oven glass dishes such as Wear-ever™, Anchor Hocking™ and Pyrex™ should be used for indirect cooking only.*

12. Skillet. Any skillet that is entirely grill-safe (ovenproof and flame-proof) can be used for frying and baking. A skillet can also be used in place of a griddle.

13. Meat thermometer. Insert a meat thermometer in large cuts of meat and whole poultry to determine doneness.

14. Oven thermometer. Always place an oven thermometer over the unlit burner when indirect cooking to determine the temperature inside the grill. You will need to adjust the heat setting when indirect cooking to maintain the correct temperature.

15. Metal and wooden skewers. Prepare grilled kabobs on metal or wooden skewers. Use wooden skewers when you are preparing kabobs that have a short cooking time. Soak them in water for about 30 minutes before adding food so they do not burn when placed on the hot cooking grid.

How to Direct Cook

This quick grilling method is ideal for foods like burgers, kabobs and chicken pieces. Meats get great grilled flavor as juices drip onto the rocks and create smoke. If flare-ups occur, rearrange the food and turn down the heat. Cook with the hood open or closed. When the hood is closed, the grill keeps a more even cooking temperature and uses less energy. Food cooks faster and there are fewer flare-ups.

Cooking grid. Arrange the food on the cooking grid over the preheated lava rocks.

Lava rock grate. Cook directly on the lava rock grate just like you do on the rangetop. Before turning on the grill, place the pan or dish on the grate, arranging the rocks around the pan.

How to Rotisserie Cook

Use the rotisserie accessory to cook large cuts of meat and whole poultry. As the spit slowly turns, meats baste in their own juices, making the final product moist and flavorful. Keep the hood closed when cooking on the rotisserie. This holds heat inside the grill and helps food cook and brown evenly.

Select meats that are evenly shaped for uniform cooking.

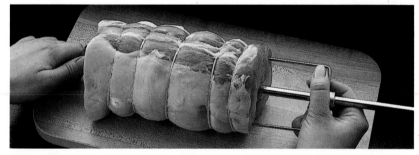

Skewer meat on the spit and secure with metal prongs. Meat should be balanced and centered so it cooks evenly and does not overwork the rotisserie motor.

Check balance by holding the spit across your palms. Rotate the spit; it should rotate easily and evenly. If balance is off, remove the meat and re-position it on spit.

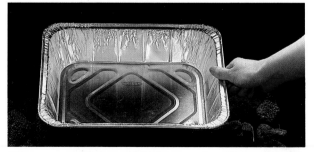

Remove cooking grid before preheating grill. Place a shallow drip pan directly on the lava rocks to catch juices that drip from meat during grilling.

How to Indirect Cook

You can bake and roast foods in your gas grill just as you do in a conventional oven. Casseroles, whole poultry, breads and cakes cook by this indirect method. As the name implies, the food is not grilled directly over the hot lava rocks. Instead, it cooks by hot air circulating inside the grill.

Single-burner grill. Cover half the cooking grid with a double thickness of heavy-duty aluminum foil, or invert a baking pan over half the grid. Preheat the grill, then place food on the covered grid.

Two-burner grill. Preheat the grill, then turn off one burner. Place food on the grid over the unlit burner.

Oven thermometer. Place an oven thermometer over the unlit side of the grill when indirect cooking. Regulate the heat setting as needed to maintain the desired baking temperature.

Grill hood. Always indirect cook with the hood closed to keep heat inside the grill.

Temperature Guide (indirect heat)

Use this guide when you bake or roast your own favorite dishes in your gas grill. Use the baking temperature recommended in your recipe to determine the correct heat setting. If you are grilling on a very cold or hot day, you may need to adjust the heat setting to maintain the correct baking temperature.

BAKING TEMPERATURE	HEAT SETTING	ITEM
250° to 300°F	LOW	Smoked foods, warming rolls and leftovers
325° to 375°F	MEDIUM	Roasts, meat loaves, ribs, fish, poultry, casseroles, vegetables, cakes, bars, pies, cookies
400° to 450°F	HIGH	Biscuits, rolls, pizza

Smoke Cooking

Hickory-smoked meats, poultry and fish are easy and delicious when prepared on the gas grill. (Smoke cooking works best on a two-burner grill.) Use wood chips wrapped in foil logs for smoke cooking. Hickory chips give meats that distinct smoked flavor. Try woods like pecan, walnut, cherry or apple for other unique flavors. Follow the directions below for making a foil log with wood chips. You will need several foil logs each time you smoke cook.

Smoke Cooking Guide

Item	Whole Fish 4 to 5 lbs.	Pork Spareribs 4 lbs.	Beef Chuck Roast 2 to 3 lbs. 1¼ in. thick
Cooking Time	1 to 1½ hrs.	1 to 2 hrs.	45 min. to 1½ hrs.

How to Make a Foil Log

Place dried wood chips in water to soak at least 1 hour before you grill. The amount of chips you need depends on how long you will be smoke cooking (usually a few pounds). Keep the chips soaking as you smoke cook, draining chips as you need them for foil logs.

Begin with an 18-inch square of heavy-duty aluminum foil. Fold it in half to form an 18×9-inch rectangle.

How to Prepare the Grill for Smoke Cooking

Remove the cooking grid before preheating the grill. Move all the lava rocks onto one half of the grate.

Preheat grill for 10 minutes. Place one foil log directly on hot lava rocks. Place a shallow drip pan filled with 1 to 2 inches water on empty half of lava rock grate. Replace cooking grid over drip pan.

12

Drain about 2 cups soaked wood chips just before you are ready to grill. Place them in center of foil rectangle. Bring the shorter edges of rectangle together over chips. Fold down several times to make a tight seam.

Leave ends of log open so smoke can flow from the log and circulate inside the grill during smoke cooking.

Close grill hood. Leave heat setting at HIGH for 10 to 20 minutes, or until the wood chips ignite.

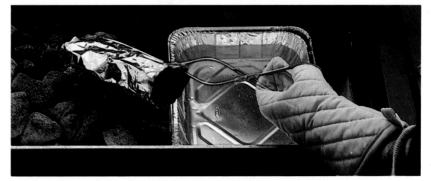

Turn off burner under drip pan. Turn the heat setting to LOW under the lava rocks. Place the food on the cooking grid over the drip pan and close the hood. Replace foil logs as needed during cooking to maintain continuous smoking.

Foil Wrapping

Wrap and grill foods in foil packets for fast preparation and easy clean-up. Use the drugstore wrap for foods which need to be turned over frequently, such as flat cuts of meat or loose vegetables. Use the bundle wrap for foods which do not require turning over and are too bulky to be drugstore wrapped. The bundle wrap also lets you easily check the food for doneness. A drugstore wrap is more difficult to open and reclose if further cooking is needed. Use heavy-duty aluminum foil for these packets to lessen the chance of burning the food.

How to Drugstore Wrap

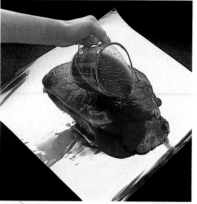  

Center food on large sheet of heavy-duty aluminum foil. Foil should be large enough to enclose food and allow for folding.

Bring edges together over food and fold down several times. Leave space around food so hot air can circulate in packet.

Fold short ends several times toward food. Crimp ends tightly to prevent leaking.

How to Bundle Wrap

Center food on large square of heavy-duty aluminum foil. Foil should be at least three times the size of the food.

Bring four corners together over food. Fold corners down to seal. Allow room inside the packet for heat circulation.

Crimp each seam and fold over to seal. This prevents steam which forms inside the packet from escaping so foods cook faster and more evenly.

Cleaning the Grill

Lava rocks may become coated with food juices and cooking sauces which do not burn off during preheating. This may make foods cook unevenly, or cause flare-ups and smoking. To remove this stubborn coating, remove the cooking grid from a cool grill. Turn the lava rocks over. Replace the cooking grid. Set the grill at HIGH and close the hood. After 15 to 20 minutes, the food residue will have burned off. Turn off the grill and let it cool. The grill is ready for your next cookout. Also, clean the inside of the grill and the burner at least once a year. Follow the directions for this procedure in your grill use and care manual.

Fat on meats and poultry will partially melt during grilling. Most of this fat flows into the grease container under the back of the grill. When the container is full, empty it or replace it with a new container. Fats may also accumulate around the edge of the cooking grid. Clean this area periodically so it doesn't become a fire hazard.

Cooking grid should be cleaned after each cookout so your grill is always ready to use. When you clean the grid, the grill should be turned off, but still warm. Scrub the grid with a stiff wire brush to remove the burned-on food residue. (A brush with brass wire bristles works best.) You can also use mild soap and hot water to clean the grid, if desired. Rinse and dry the grid thoroughly before replacing it on the grill. A small grid can be cleaned in the dishwasher. *Never* use a commercial oven cleaner to clean the cooking grid. This could leave a harmful coating on the grid which might transfer onto grilled food.

Outside of the grill should be occasionally washed and oiled. After washing it with mild soap and water, rinse and allow it to dry. Lightly coat the surface with vegetable oil. Close the hood and heat grill at HIGH for 15 minutes. This will season the surface of the grill and keep it looking its best.

Breakfast Menus

Surprise friends or family with breakfast on the grill. Potted Peppers (right) are unique, yet easy and fast to prepare. Make toast by placing a few slices of bread on the preheated cooking grid for about 1 minute, turning over once. Or prepare a hearty breakfast of pancakes and sausage on a griddle or skillet. To warm the syrup, place it in a grill-safe bowl and set it on the edge of the cooking grid or upper cooking rack to warm.

Company Breakfast ▲

Potted Peppers, *p.68*

Hash Brown Potatoes

Toast

Juice

Coffee

About an hour before breakfast, begin grilling the Potted Peppers. While the peppers finish cooking, fry the frozen hash brown potatoes on the other half of the grill according to package directions. Toast a few slices of bread on the cooking grid just before serving.

◄Hearty Breakfast

Pancakes, *p.85*

Sausage, *p.49*

Syrup

Juice

Coffee

The night before, prepare and refrigerate the pancake batter. Begin grilling the sausages and pancakes about 15 minutes before serving. At this time, warm the syrup on the edge of the cooking grid or on the upper cooking rack.

Brunch Menus

Brunch is usually served in place of breakfast and lunch, so plan to serve generous portions of a variety of foods. Set your table outside so you can serve dishes like Spiced Cider (left) and Fruit Kabobs (below) directly from the grill. Display the other dishes on the grill shelf or a nearby table. Make a schedule the night before so all the food will be ready to serve at the same time.

Autumn Brunch ▲

Cheesy Sausage Bake, *p. 69*

Cinnamon Monkey Bread, *p. 86*

Hot Spiced Cider, *p. 80*

The day before the brunch, prepare and bake the bread. About 45 minutes before serving time, begin baking the Cheesy Sausage Bake on half the grill. Place the pot of cider on the other half of the grill and heat for about 20 minutes.

Quiche 'n Kabob Brunch ▶

Mini Quiches Lorraine, *p. 83*

Polynesian Kabobs, *p. 81*

Hawaiian Fruit Kabobs, *p. 73*

Juice

Coffee

Early in the day, assemble and refrigerate the quiche crusts and kabobs. Begin baking the quiches 40 to 50 minutes before brunch. When they finish baking, cover them with aluminum foil to keep warm. Begin grilling the kabobs 10 to 15 minutes before serving time.

Lunch Menus

For a change of pace prepare your lunch outside on the grill. If you're having guests, try the Submarine Sandwich (opposite). Assemble it in the morning before your guests arrive. Everyday favorites like grilled cheese sandwiches or pizza take on new excitement when you make them on the grill. And what can beat a perfectly-grilled burger for satisfying lunchtime appetites?

Family Favorite Lunch ▲

Deluxe Grilled Cheese Sandwiches, *p. 68*

French Fries

Coleslaw

Chocolate Chip Oatmeal Cookies, *p. 92*

The day before or early in the day, bake the cookies, and prepare and refrigerate the coleslaw. About 30 minutes before lunch, bake the frozen French fries according to package directions. Keep the fries warm over the unlit burner on the grill while you cook the sandwiches on the griddle over the other half.

◄ Pizzeria Lunch

Deep Dish Skillet Pizza, *p. 48*

Tossed Salad

Early in the day, prepare and refrigerate the pizza sauce. Assemble and begin baking the pizza about 70 minutes before lunchtime. Prepare the salad while the pizza bakes. Toss salad with desired dressing just before serving.

Do Ahead Lunch ▲

Hot Hero Sandwich, *p.45*

Chips

Relishes

Brownies, *p.93*

Prepare the entire meal in the morning, so at lunchtime all you need to do is heat the sandwich. Bake the brownies and set aside to cool before frosting. Arrange the relishes on a tray. Cover and refrigerate until serving time. Put the sandwich together, wrap it in aluminum foil and refrigerate. Place it on the upper cooking rack to heat about 15 minutes before lunch.

Beans and Burger Lunch ▶

Creamy Horseradish Burgers, *p.28*

Toasted Bratwurst Buns

Baked Beans, *p.75*

Several hours before lunch, shape the burgers. Cover with plastic wrap and refrigerate. Begin baking the beans about an hour before lunch. Keep them warm on half the grid while you grill the burgers on the other half. Place bratwurst buns on the grid beside the burgers for the last few minutes of grilling so they will be warm and toasted by serving time.

19

Dinner Menus

A grilled dinner can be as enjoyable to make as it is to eat. Don't cook just the meat on the grill. Save time and energy by grilling the entire meal. Plan an interesting menu by including a variety of flavors, colors and textures. Keep your eyes open for bargains on seasonal vegetables like squash and corn on the cob. These can save you money as well as add special flavors to your menus.

Sparerib Cookout ▲

Hickory-Smoked Spareribs, *p.38*

Herbed Potatoes and Carrots, *p.74*

Coleslaw

Several hours before dinner, prepare and refrigerate the coleslaw, the foil packet of potatoes and carrots, and the sauce for the ribs. Start grilling the ribs 1½ hours before serving. Place the vegetable packet on the cooking grid beside the ribs 20 to 25 minutes before dinner.

◄Dressed-Up Favorites

Broccoli-Mushroom Meatloaf, *p.29*

Cauliflower, *p.77*

Tossed Salad

Hot Dinner Rolls

Early in the day, prepare and refrigerate the salad ingredients and the meatloaf. Start grilling the meatloaf 1½ hours before dinner. After about 30 minutes, add the cauliflower. Wrap the rolls in aluminum foil and place on the upper cooking rack to heat for 5 to 10 minutes. Toss the salad with your favorite dressing just before serving.

Super Summer Supper ▲

Sweet-and-Spicy Chicken, *p.53*

Corn on the Cob, *p.76, 77*

Fruit Salad

Hot Dinner Rolls

In the morning, make and refrigerate the fruit salad and the sauce for the chicken. Begin grilling the chicken 30 to 45 minutes before dinner. Add the corn after 10 to 20 minutes. About 10 minutes before serving, wrap rolls in aluminum foil and place on the upper cooking rack to heat.

Supper on a Skewer ▶

Sirloin Kabobs, *p.31*

Hot Cooked Rice

Asparagus, *p.77*

Early in the day, assemble and refrigerate the kabobs. About 20 minutes before serving, cook the rice and begin grilling the packet of asparagus. After 5 minutes, add the kabobs to the grill. When the rice finishes cooking, place it on the edge of the grid to keep warm until dinner.

Special Menus

Let your grill help create a memorable meal for your next special occasion. For an elegant menu, serve a tall Crown Roast of Pork stuffed with apricots and cranberries (opposite). For something simpler but just as delicious, try Spaghetti and Cheesy Herb French Bread (opposite). This menu would be ideal for a large crowd. Let guests serve themselves right from the grill.

Summer Cookout ▲

Basic Steak, *p.27*

Mushrooms, *p.77*

Bacon-Wrapped Baked Potatoes, *p.74*

Greek-Style Zucchini *p.76*

Fruit-Filled Pie *p.91*

Early in the day, bake the pie. Assemble and refrigerate the mushrooms, potatoes and zucchini. About 1 hour before serving, begin baking the potatoes. After 30 minutes, add the zucchini and begin grilling the steaks. Add the packet of mushrooms about 10 minutes before the meal is served.

◄Seafarer's Supper

Seafood Kabobs, *p.59*

Rice Pilaf, *p.76*

Green Beans, *p.77*

Several hours before grilling, assemble and refrigerate the kabobs. About 40 minutes before serving, prepare the rice and begin grilling the packet of beans. After 20 minutes, remove the rice and beans. Cover with aluminum foil to keep warm. Place kabobs on cooking grid to grill.

Elegant Autumn Dinner ▲

Crown Roast of Pork, *p.37*

Marshmallow Yam Bake, *p.76*

Applesauce Cake, *p.91*

In the morning, bake the cake. Set it aside to cool before frosting. Begin grilling the roast 3½ hours before serving time. Add the Marshmallow Yam Bake to the grill about 30 minutes before dinner.

Zesty Italian Dinner ▶

Spaghetti Sauce, *p.47*

Hot Cooked Spaghetti

Cheesy Herb French Bread, *p.87*

Tossed Salad

Fudgy Coconut Pie, *p.89*

Early in the day, bake the pie and prepare the salad ingredients. Assemble and refrigerate the bread. Begin cooking the spaghetti sauce 1½ hours before dinner. After about 1 hour, cook the spaghetti and place the bread on the upper cooking rack to heat.

Meats &
Main Dishes

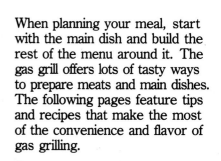

When planning your meal, start with the main dish and build the rest of the menu around it. The gas grill offers lots of tasty ways to prepare meats and main dishes. The following pages feature tips and recipes that make the most of the convenience and flavor of gas grilling.

For easy preparation, fast clean-up and energy efficiency, plan an entire meal on the grill. Start with a quick-to-fix main dish like juicy pork chops. Add a foil packet of vegetables and a pan of fresh rolls. Complete the meal with a light dessert such as grilled fresh fruit.

Let your gas grill take the fuss out of entertaining. For a large crowd, try Sirloin Kabobs. Cut up the meat and vegetables in advance, then let your guests skewer their own combinations. For a smaller get-together, serve a big Hot Hero Sandwich. Or try Elegant Oriental Veal for a special occasion.

Each of the following sections begins with helpful tips for selecting and preparing meats. Let the recipes get you started. The more you use your gas grill, the more ways you'll discover to create wonderful main dishes!

Deep Dish Skillet Pizza, page 48

Beef

Grilled steaks and hamburgers are favorites of almost everyone who enjoys outdoor cooking. The robust flavor of barbecued beef makes it easy to see why. But there's more to grilling than steaks and burgers. Although these are the quickest and easiest to prepare, other types of beef are great on the grill, too. Even inexpensive cuts turn out moist and tender with the aid of marinades, sauces and bastes. Chuck roast, brisket and short ribs are just a few of the many beef cuts that can be grilled with delicious results.

Cooking times for the beef recipes on the following pages are for medium doneness. If you prefer your beef rare or well-done, adjust the cooking times slightly.

Do not cut or pierce beef to check for doneness. Instead, use the touch test. Lightly press your finger on the center of the steak or burger (see doneness test, opposite), being careful not to burn your finger. If the meat is too hot to touch, press the back of a spoon on the meat. Use this handy test for juicy, flavorful steaks or burgers.

Tips for Grilling Beef

Trim large pieces of fat from steaks and roasts. (Use these to season the cooking grid.) If the large pieces are not removed, they will melt during grilling and drip onto the lava rocks, creating flare-ups.

Leave a small layer of fat around the edges of steaks and roasts to add flavor and moisture to meat. Slash at 1½-inch intervals to keep the edges from curling during cooking. Do not cut into the meat as flavorful juices could be lost.

Use tongs to handle meat on the grill after it has been seared. Do not pierce it with a knife or fork. If flare-ups occur, rearrange meat to prevent burning. Do not use water to extinguish flare-ups.

How to Test Meat for Doneness: Touch Test

Rare meat gives easily when touched. It is seared, but no juices appear on the surface.

Medium meat feels firmer yet slightly springy, and juices begin to appear on the surface.

Well-done meat is covered with juices. It is firm and does not yield to pressure.

Basic Steak
pictured opposite

4 T-bone steaks, 1½ inches thick, about 1½ lbs. each

Seasoning for Beef, page 63 (optional)

Preheat grill for 10 minutes. Trim large pieces of fat from steaks. Make vertical slashes in fat around edges at 1½-inch intervals to keep edges from curling. Arrange steaks 2 inches apart on cooking grid. Sprinkle with Seasoning for Beef. Grill at MEDIUM with hood closed until steaks feel slightly firm,* 25 to 30 minutes, turning over once.   *4 servings*

*Touch test, above.

TIP: Rearrange steaks several times during grilling to prevent flare-ups.

▲Creamy Horseradish Burgers

2 lbs. ground beef
2 tablespoons steak sauce
¾ teaspoon seasoned salt
1 pkg. (3 oz.) cream
   cheese, softened
1 to 2 tablespoons prepared
   horseradish
1 teaspoon prepared mustard
6 bratwurst buns or hard rolls
   Lettuce leaves
   Tomato slices

Preheat grill for 10 minutes. In medium mixing bowl, combine ground beef, steak sauce and seasoned salt. Mix well. Shape into 12 thin oval patties, each about 6 inches long.

In small bowl, blend cream cheese, horseradish and mustard. Spread about 1 tablespoon in center of each of 6 patties. Top with remaining patties. Press edges to seal. Grill at MEDIUM with hood closed until burgers feel slightly firm,* 10 to 14 minutes, turning over once. Serve in bratwurst buns with lettuce and tomato.

6 servings

*Touch test, page 27.

Basic Hamburgers

1½ lbs. ground beef
2 tablespoons French
   dressing
¼ teaspoon salt
⅛ teaspoon pepper
   Seasoning for Beef,
   page 63 (optional)

Preheat grill for 10 minutes. In medium mixing bowl, combine all ingredients except Seasoning for Beef. Mix well. Shape into six 3½-inch diameter patties. Grill at MEDIUM with hood closed until burgers feel slightly firm,* 10 to 14 minutes, turning over once and sprinkling with Seasoning for Beef.

Double Cheese Burgers: Follow recipe above, omitting salt. Shape ground beef mixture into twelve 3½-inch diameter patties. Place a thin slice of American process cheese food spread on each of 6 patties. Top with remaining patties. Press edges together to seal. Grill as directed. Top each burger with another thin slice of American process cheese during last minute of grilling.   *6 servings*

*Touch test, page 27.

Meat and Potato Patties

1 lb. ground beef
½ cup grated, peeled potato
⅓ cup finely-chopped fresh
   mushrooms
3 tablespoons finely-chopped
   onion
1 egg, slightly beaten
1 teaspoon dried parsley
   flakes
½ teaspoon salt
¼ teaspoon pepper

Season grid with vegetable oil. Preheat grill for 10 minutes. In medium mixing bowl, mix all ingredients. Shape into six 3½-inch diameter patties.

Grill patties at MEDIUM with hood closed until patties feel slightly firm,* 10 to 16 minutes, turning over once.   *6 servings*

*Touch test, page 27.

Broccoli-Mushroom Meatloaf

Meatloaf:
1½ lbs. ground beef
⅓ cup seasoned dry
    bread crumbs
¼ cup milk
1 egg
1 teaspoon Worcestershire
    sauce
1 teaspoon instant minced
    onion
¾ teaspoon salt
½ teaspoon ground sage
¼ teaspoon pepper

Filling:
1 pkg. (10 oz.) frozen
    chopped broccoli, thawed
1 can (4 oz.) sliced
    mushrooms, drained

Preheat grill for 10 minutes.
Continue as directed below.

6 servings

How to Make Broccoli-Mushroom Meatloaf

Combine all meatloaf ingredients in medium mixing bowl. Mix well. Place mixture in center of 20-inch long sheet of wax paper.

Pat mixture into 15 × 9-inch rectangle. Sprinkle with broccoli and mushrooms, leaving a 1½-inch border. Roll up tightly, starting with shorter edge, using wax paper to lift.

Press edges and end of roll to seal. Place seam-side down in 9 × 5-inch grill-safe loaf pan. Bake using indirect MEDIUM heat with hood closed until well browned, 60 to 70 minutes.

◄Chuck Roast with Vegetables

3 lb. beef chuck roast, 2 to 2½ inches thick
   Meat tenderizer
   Pepper
4 small potatoes
1 medium onion, sliced
2 stalks celery, cut into 3-inch pieces
2 medium carrots, cut into 3-inch pieces
2 cloves garlic
⅓ cup water, beer or tomato juice
1 teaspoon dried parsley flakes
½ teaspoon instant beef bouillon granules
¼ teaspoon dried thyme leaves

Preheat grill for 10 minutes. Pierce roast several times with fork. Sprinkle both sides with meat tenderizer and pepper. Pound with meat mallet.* Grill roast at MEDIUM with hood closed until well seared, about 20 minutes, turning over once. Place in grill-safe baking dish or on 24 × 18-inch double thickness of heavy-duty aluminum foil.

Pierce potatoes. Arrange potatoes, onion, celery, carrots and garlic around meat. In small bowl, mix water, parsley flakes, bouillon granules and thyme. Pour over meat and vegetables. Cover or drugstore wrap (page 14).

Bake using indirect MEDIUM heat until roast is tender, 60 to 65 minutes.   *6 servings*

*If desired, marinate roast in Italian Marinade or Tomato Beer Marinade, page 65, instead of sprinkling with meat tenderizer and pepper.

Seasoned Tip Roast

2 tablespoons dried parsley flakes
4 cloves garlic, minced
1 teaspoon dried rosemary leaves
½ teaspoon dried thyme leaves
¼ teaspoon ground pepper
5 lb. beef sirloin tip roast
   Cracked pepper
   Hard rolls

In small bowl, combine parsley flakes, garlic, rosemary, thyme and ground pepper. Cut about 20 slits in roast, 2 inches deep and 1½ inches long. Stuff a small amount of mixture into each slit. For stronger flavor, cover and refrigerate for about 8 hours.

Remove cooking grid. Center drip pan directly on lava rocks. Rub roast with cracked pepper. Skewer and balance roast on spit. Rotiss at MEDIUM until internal temperature is 150°F, 1¼ to 1½ hours. Thinly slice and serve with hard rolls.

8 to 10 servings

Barbecued Beef Brisket

3½ lb. beef brisket
1 can (12 oz.) cola
2 cups barbecue sauce
1 stick cinnamon
2 whole cloves
4 whole peppercorns
   Hamburger buns

Place brisket in shallow glass baking dish or large plastic food storage bag. Pour cola over brisket. Cover dish or close bag. Refrigerate for at least 8 hours, turning brisket over after half the time.

Preheat grill for 10 minutes. Remove brisket from cola. Place on 24 × 18-inch double thickness of heavy-duty aluminum foil. Pour barbecue sauce over brisket. Add cinnamon stick, cloves and peppercorns. Drugstore wrap, (page 14). Bake using indirect MEDIUM heat until tender, about 2 hours. Slice and serve with barbecue sauce and buns.

6 to 8 servings

Fruited Short Ribs ▶

4 lbs. beef short ribs
1 recipe Pineapple Curry
   Marinade, page 65

1 pkg. (8 oz.) dried mixed
   fruit (1½ cups)
1 small onion, sliced

Place ribs in shallow glass baking dish or large plastic food storage
bag. Prepare marinade as directed. Pour over ribs. Cover dish or
close bag. Refrigerate for at least 8 hours, turning ribs over
occasionally.

Preheat grill for 10 minutes. Remove ribs. Strain and reserve
marinade. Grill ribs at MEDIUM with hood closed until well
seared, 10 to 15 minutes, turning over frequently. Place ribs in
grill-safe baking dish. Add fruit, onion and reserved marinade.
Cover. Bake using indirect MEDIUM heat until ribs are tender, 1
to 1½ hours. Remove fruit and onion with a slotted spoon and
serve with ribs. *4 servings*

◐ Sirloin Kabobs

1 recipe Seasoned Butter
   Baste, page 64
1½ lbs. boneless beef
   sirloin, 1 inch thick, cut
   into 1½-inch pieces

1 medium green pepper,
   cut into 1½-inch pieces
8 large fresh mushrooms
8 cherry tomatoes

Preheat grill for 10 minutes. Prepare baste as directed and set
aside. Alternate beef, green pepper and mushrooms on four 12 to
14-inch skewers.

Place kabobs on cooking grid. Brush with baste. Grill at MEDIUM
with hood closed until well seared, 10 to 15 minutes, turning over and
brushing with baste several times. Add cherry tomatoes to skewers
during last 2 minutes of grilling. *4 servings*

Italian Beef Kabobs

1½ lbs. boneless beef top
   round steak, cut into
   4 × 1 × ½-inch strips
4 new potatoes

1 zucchini, 1½-inch
   diameter, cut into
   ½-inch slices
1 recipe Italian
   Marinade, page 65

Place beef strips in shallow glass baking dish or large plastic food
storage bag. Cut potatoes in half. Parboil for 10 minutes. Drain.
Add to beef. Prepare marinade as directed. Pour over steak and
potatoes. Cover dish or close bag. Refrigerate for at least 4 hours,
turning steak and potatoes once.

Preheat grill for 10 minutes. Remove meat and potatoes from
marinade. Alternate beef, potatoes and zucchini on four 12 to
14-inch skewers. Grill at MEDIUM with hood closed until well
seared, 10 to 15 minutes, turning over frequently. *4 servings*

Sukiyaki

3 tablespoons vegetable oil
¼ cup chopped green onion
1 medium green pepper,
    cut into 1-inch pieces
1 to 1½ lbs. boneless beef
    sirloin steak, cut into
    thin strips
1½ cups fresh bean sprouts,
    or 1 can (16 oz.) bean
    sprouts, drained
1 can (8 oz.) sliced water
    chestnuts, drained
6 cherry tomatoes, cut in
    half

Sauce:

¼ cup water
2 tablespoons soy sauce
2 teaspoons cornstarch
¼ teaspoon ground ginger
¼ teaspoon salt
¼ teaspoon pepper

Hot cooked rice

4 to 6 servings

How to Make Sukiyaki

Remove cooking grid. Before lighting grill, place large cast-iron skillet or grill-safe baking dish directly on lava rock grate. Arrange rocks around skillet. If your grill has two burners, cook over one burner only.

Place oil in skillet. Cook at MEDIUM-HIGH until hot, about 1 minute. Add onion and green pepper. Stir-fry until vegetables are tender-crisp, 2 to 3 minutes.

Add beef. Cook and stir until beef is no longer pink. Add bean sprouts, water chestnuts and tomatoes. Cook with hood closed for 2 to 3 minutes.

Blend water, soy sauce, cornstarch, ginger, salt and pepper in small bowl. Add to beef and vegetable mixture.

Cook and stir with hood open until thickened and bubbly, 2 to 3 minutes. Spread rice on serving platter. Spoon sukiyaki onto rice.

Tacos ▲

1 lb. ground beef
⅓ cup chopped onion
2 tablespoons finely-
    chopped black olives
1 teaspoon ground cumin
½ teaspoon salt
¼ teaspoon garlic powder
⅛ teaspoon pepper
12 taco shells
½ cup seeded, chopped tomato

Toppings:
    Guacamole
    Chopped green onion
    Grated Cheddar cheese
    Shredded lettuce

Preheat grill for 10 minutes.* In large cast-iron skillet or grill-safe baking dish, combine ground beef and onion. Cook and stir at HIGH with hood open until beef is no longer pink, 10 to 12 minutes. Drain. Stir in olives, cumin, salt, garlic powder and pepper. Place taco shells on upper cooking rack. Cook meat mixture with hood closed for about 5 minutes longer. Stir in tomato. Reduce heat setting to LOW and serve from grill with toppings. *12 tacos*

*If your grill has two burners, preheat and cook over one burner only.

Chili

1½ lbs. coarse-ground beef
1 cup chopped onion
2 slices bacon, chopped
2 cloves garlic, cut in half
2 cans (16 oz. each) whole
    tomatoes, undrained
2 cans (15½ oz. each)
    kidney beans, drained
¾ cup water
1 can (6 oz.) tomato paste
2½ tablespoons chili powder
1½ teaspoons salt
1 teaspoon ground cumin
¼ teaspoon pepper
⅛ teaspoon cayenne

In 5-quart cast-iron pot or grill-safe baking dish, combine ground beef, onion, bacon and garlic. Remove cooking grid. Place pot directly on lava rock grate, arranging rocks around pot.* Cook and stir at HIGH with hood open until beef is no longer pink, 10 to 15 minutes. Add remaining ingredients. Stir to blend and break apart tomatoes. Cover. Reduce heat to LOW. Cook with hood closed until chili is desired consistency, 45 to 60 minutes, stirring 2 or 3 times. *8 servings*

*If your grill has two burners, cook over one burner only.

Liver Skillet Dinner

⅓ cup all-purpose flour
½ teaspoon poultry seasoning
¼ teaspoon pepper
1 lb. beef liver, cut into
    4 × 1 × ½-inch strips
6 slices bacon
2 medium onions, thinly
    sliced, separated into
    rings
1 tablespoon vegetable oil

Place flour, poultry seasoning and pepper in plastic food storage bag. Add liver. Shake to coat. Remove liver from bag.

Remove cooking grid. Place large cast-iron skillet or grill-safe baking dish directly on lava rock grate, arranging rocks around skillet.* Place bacon in skillet. Fry at MEDIUM-HIGH with hood closed until bacon is crisp, turning over once. Remove bacon. Set aside.

Reduce heat to MEDIUM. Place onion in skillet. Cook until tender. Push to one side of skillet. Add oil and liver. Cook until liver is brown, 6 to 10 minutes, turning over once. Top with onion and bacon.

4 servings

*If your grill has two burners, cook over one burner only.

Beef Cooking Guide

ITEM	HEAT SETTING	COOKING TIME (for medium doneness)	METHOD
Hamburgers:			
¼ lb. each ½ in. thick	MEDIUM	12 to 14 min.	Preheat grill for 10 minutes. Grill burgers with hood closed. Turn over once.
Steaks:			
T-bone or Porterhouse 1 to 1½ lbs. each 1 in. thick 1½ in. thick	MEDIUM	8 to 10 min. 25 to 30 min.	Preheat grill for 10 minutes. Trim excess fat from steaks. Grill with hood closed. Turn steaks over once.
Sirloin 2 to 3 lbs. 1½ in. thick 4 to 6 servings	MEDIUM	18 to 20 min.	Preheat grill for 10 minutes. Trim excess fat from steak. Grill with hood closed. Turn steak over once.
Top Round 2 to 3 lbs. 1½ in. thick 4 to 6 servings	MEDIUM	20 to 25 min.	Marinate or tenderize.* Preheat grill for 10 minutes. Grill steak with hood closed. Turn over once.
Flank 1½ lbs. ¾ in. thick 4 servings	HIGH	12 to 15 min.	Marinate or tenderize.* Preheat grill for 10 minutes. Score steak with diamond pattern. Grill with hood closed. Turn steak over once.
Roasts:			
Pot Roast or Chuck Roast 3 lbs. 1½ in. thick 6 to 8 servings	MEDIUM	20 min. to sear 1 to 1½ hrs. to cook	Marinate or tenderize.* Preheat grill for 10 minutes. Sear roast, turning over once. Place in grill-safe baking dish or on double thickness of heavy-duty aluminum foil. Cover or wrap tightly. Grill using indirect heat with hood closed.
Sirloin Tip 4 to 5 lbs. 8 to 10 servings	MEDIUM	1 to 1½ hrs. to cook	Remove cooking grid. Center drip pan directly on lava rocks. Rotiss roast with hood closed. (Roast should reach internal temperature of 150°F.)
Ribs:			
Beef Short Ribs 4 lbs. 4 servings	MEDIUM	20 to 30 min. to sear 1 to 1½ hrs. to cook	Preheat grill for 10 minutes. Sear ribs, turning over several times. Place in grill-safe baking dish or on double thickness of heavy-duty aluminum foil. Add 2 cups barbecue sauce. Cover or wrap tightly. Grill using indirect heat with hood closed.

Refrigerate beef in desired marinade, page 64 or 65. Or tenderize beef by sprinkling with meat tenderizer and pounding with meat mallet.

Pork

Barbecued spareribs have always been a popular meat to prepare on the grill. You can get great grilled results from other pork cuts, too. Pork roasts, fresh or smoked chops and ham slices are also delicious. Choose thick chops, steaks and ham slices for juicy, tender results. A one-inch thick cut works best for grilling.

Pork should be cooked to 170°F. Use a meat thermometer to determine when large, thick cuts reach this temperature. Insert the thermometer before grilling. At the end of the suggested cooking time, check the temperature in several places to make sure the meat is thoroughly cooked. Do not let the thermometer touch bone. This could make the temperature reading incorrect.

Make a small cut in the center or near the bone to check for doneness in thin cuts like chops and steaks. When pork is done, the juices run clear and the meat is no longer pink. Most hams and smoked chops are already fully cooked. Just sear and heat them through before serving.

Sauerkraut-Stuffed Pork Roast

5 lb. boneless pork loin
  roast
1 can (16 oz.) sauerkraut,
  rinsed and drained

2 tablespoons packed
  brown sugar
1/2 teaspoon caraway seed
1/4 cup plum jelly, melted
  (optional)

Untie roast. Separate halves and set aside, fat-side down. In small mixing bowl, mix sauerkraut, brown sugar and caraway seed. Press onto one half of roast. Place other half, fat-side up, on top. Tie with string in several places.

Remove cooking grid. Center drip pan directly on lava rocks. Skewer and balance roast on spit. Rotiss at LOW with hood closed until internal temperature reaches 170°F, 2¼ to 3 hours, brushing with jelly during last 30 minutes of cooking.   *8 to 10 servings*

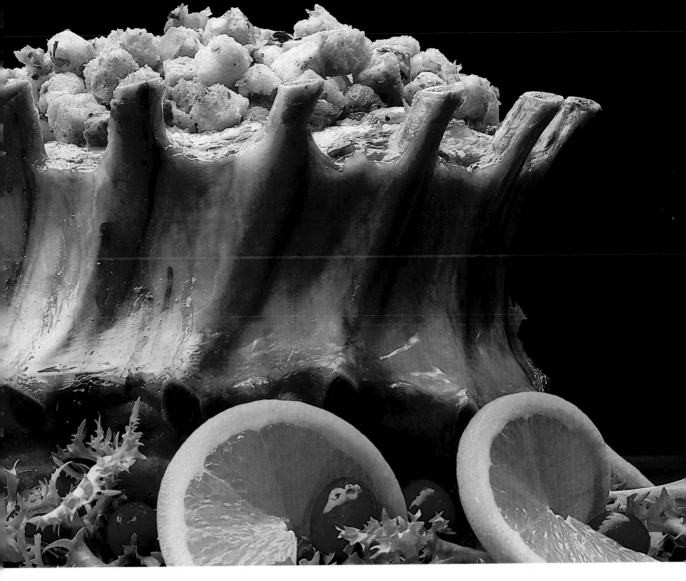

Crown Roast of Pork ▲

5 cups unseasoned croutons
1 can (8 oz.) apricot halves,
    drained and chopped
1 cup chopped celery
¾ cup chopped onion
¾ cup water
½ cup snipped fresh parsley
½ cup chopped cranberries
⅓ cup butter or margarine
2 tablespoons honey
1 teaspoon salt
1 teaspoon dried marjoram
    leaves
1 teaspoon poultry seasoning
1 teaspoon grated orange peel
1 teaspoon instant chicken
    bouillon granules
¼ teaspoon pepper
9 to 10 lb. pork crown roast

Place croutons in medium mixing bowl. Set aside. In 2-quart grill-safe saucepan, combine remaining ingredients except roast. Mix well. Remove cooking grid. Place saucepan directly on lava rock grate, arranging rocks around pan.* Cook at HIGH with hood open until mixture boils. Cover and reduce heat to LOW. Simmer with hood closed for 5 minutes. Remove from heat. Pour over croutons. Mix well. Cool slightly. Cover and refrigerate.

Spread lava rocks evenly across grate with long-handled tongs. Replace cooking grid. Close hood and heat grill at HIGH for 10 minutes. Place roast, bone ends down, in grill-safe roasting pan. Bake using indirect MEDIUM heat for 1¼ hours, rotating pan once. Turn roast over. Press stuffing into center of roast. Cover stuffing with aluminum foil. Insert meat thermometer into meaty portion of roast. Bake until internal temperature reaches 170°F, 1¼ to 1¾ hours longer, rotating pan once. Let stand for 15 minutes before carving.   *8 to 10 servings*

*If your grill has two burners, cook over one burner only.

Stuffed Pork Chops▲

1 recipe Orange Spice
    Marinade, page 65
4 pork loin chops with
    pocket, 1½ inches thick
½ cup prepared mincemeat
½ cup finely-chopped apple
¼ cup finely-chopped onion

Prepare marinade as directed. Arrange pork chops in shallow glass baking dish or large plastic food storage bag. Pour marinade over chops. Cover dish or close bag. Refrigerate for at least 8 hours, turning chops over once.

Preheat grill for 5 minutes. In small mixing bowl, combine mincemeat, apple and onion. Remove chops from marinade. Press about ¼ cup stuffing mixture into each chop. Secure edges with wooden picks.

Grill chops at LOW with hood closed until no longer pink, 25 to 30 minutes, turning chops over once.   *4 servings*

Hickory-Smoked Spareribs

1 recipe Easy Barbecue
    Sauce, page 64
2½ lbs. hickory chips,
    soaked, pages 12, 13
1 can (12 oz.) beer
4 lbs. pork spareribs, cut
    into 4-rib pieces

Prepare sauce as directed. Set aside. In 12×9×3-inch aluminum pan, combine hickory chips and beer. Remove cooking grid. Center pan directly on lava rock grate, arranging rocks around pan. Replace cooking grid.

Preheat grill for 5 minutes. Arrange ribs on cooking grid above pan. Grill at LOW with hood closed until ribs are tender, 45 to 60 minutes, turning ribs over once. Brush both sides with sauce. Grill with hood closed for 20 to 30 minutes longer, turning ribs over and brushing with sauce once.   *3 or 4 servings*

Pineapple-Glazed Ham Slices

½ cup pineapple preserves
1 tablespoon soy sauce
½ teaspoon dry mustard
¼ teaspoon ground ginger
⅛ teaspoon garlic powder
1 lb. fully-cooked ham
    slices, ½ inch thick
4 slices pineapple
    (optional)

Preheat grill for 10 minutes. In small mixing bowl, combine pineapple preserves, soy sauce, mustard, ginger and garlic powder. Mix well.

Place ham slices on cooking grid. Brush with glaze. Grill at MEDIUM with hood closed until ham is seared, 8 to 10 minutes, turning over and brushing with glaze once. Grill pineapple slices for 3 to 4 minutes, turning over once. Use pineapple to garnish ham.   *2 to 4 servings*

Sweet-and-Sour Ham Kabobs▶

*1½ lbs. fully-cooked
    boneless ham, cut into
    1-inch cubes
1 jar (16 oz.) small boiled
    whole onions (24 to 30
    onions)*

*1 large green pepper, cut
    into 1-inch square pieces
1 large orange, unpeeled,
    cut into 6 wedges
½ cup sweet-and-sour
    sauce*

Preheat grill for 10 minutes. Alternate ham cubes, whole onions
and green pepper pieces on six 12 to 14-inch skewers. Add 1
orange wedge to end of each kabob. Grill at MEDIUM with hood
open until ham cubes are seared, 10 to 15 minutes, turning kabobs
over and brushing with sauce frequently.

Barbecued Ham Kabobs: Follow recipe above, substituting ½ cup
Easy Barbecue Sauce (page 64) for sweet-and-sour sauce.   *6 kabobs*

Pork Cooking Guide

ITEM	HEAT SETTING	COOKING TIME	METHOD
Bacon 4 slices	HIGH	5 to 9 min.	Preheat grill for 5 minutes.* Place seasoned griddle on cooking grid. Preheat for 5 minutes longer. Place bacon on griddle. Cook with hood open. Turn bacon over once.
Canadian Bacon 6 to 8 slices	HIGH	2 min.	(Same as above.)
Pork Chops, 4 4 to 8 oz. each ½ in. thick 1 in. thick	LOW	 15 to 20 min. 25 to 30 min.	Season cooking grid with vegetable oil. Preheat grill for 5 minutes. Grill chops with hood closed. Turn over and rearrange once.
Pork Roast (boneless) 5 lbs. 8 to 10 servings	LOW	2¼ to 3 hrs.	Remove cooking grid. Center drip pan on lava rocks. Skewer and balance roast on spit. Rotiss until internal temperature of roast reaches 170°F.
Smoked Pork Chops, 4 (fully cooked) 7 to 8 ounces each ½ inch thick	MEDIUM	10 to 15 min.	Season cooking grid with vegetable oil. Preheat grill for 10 minutes. Grill chops with hood closed. Turn over once.
Spareribs 4 lbs. 4 servings	LOW	1 to 1¼ hrs.	Preheat grill for 5 minutes. Grill ribs with hood closed. Turn over once. Brush with sauce during last 20 minutes, if desired.
Country-Style Ribs 4 lbs. 4 servings	LOW	30 to 45 min.	Parboil ribs for 20 minutes. Preheat grill for 5 minutes. Grill ribs with hood closed. Turn over once. Brush with sauce during last 20 minutes, if desired.

If your grill has two burners, preheat and cook over one burner only.

Country Ham and Biscuit Bake

⅓ cup butter or margarine
2 cups chopped onion
2 cups sliced fresh
  mushrooms
¼ cup all-purpose flour
2 tablespoons dried parsley
  flakes
1 teaspoon dried
  marjoram leaves
½ teaspoon salt
½ teaspoon pepper
1½ cups hot water
2 teaspoons instant chicken
  bouillon granules
4 cups peeled, seeded,
  coarsely-chopped
  tomatoes (about 4)
12 oz. fully-cooked boneless
  ham, cut into thin strips
  (about 3 cups)
2 cups buttermilk baking
  mix
⅔ cup milk
⅓ cup small Cheddar
  cheese cubes

6 to 8 servings

How to Make Country Ham and Biscuit Bake

Remove cooking grid. Place large cast-iron skillet or grill-safe baking dish on lava rock grate, arranging rocks around skillet. If your grill has two burners, cook over one burner only.

Place butter in skillet. Cook at MEDIUM with hood open until butter melts. Add onion and mushrooms. Cook and stir at MEDIUM until tender. Stir in flour, parsley, marjoram, salt and pepper.

Add hot water and bouillon granules. Mix well. Stir in tomatoes and ham. Cook and stir at MEDIUM with hood open until bubbly, 8 to 10 minutes. Cover and remove from heat. Set aside.

40

Spread lava rocks evenly across grate with long-handled tongs. Replace cooking grid. Close hood and heat grill at HIGH for 10 minutes.

Combine baking mix and milk in small mixing bowl. Stir just until baking mix is moistened. Stir in cheese. Drop by spoonfuls onto ham mixture to make about 8 biscuits.

Bake, uncovered, using indirect MEDIUM-HIGH heat with hood closed until biscuits are deep golden brown and filling is bubbly, 15 to 20 minutes.

Lamb & Veal

A special dinner calls for a special main dish. And nothing could be more festive than a tender cut of veal or lamb prepared on the gas grill.

Top-quality veal is pale in color. Choose thick cuts for tender, juicy results. Grill veal to medium or medium-well to bring out its mild flavor. Enhance the flavor of lamb by grilling to rare or medium. Use the touch test, page 27, to determine when steaks and chops are cooked to desired doneness. Cooking times for the following recipes are for medium doneness.

◄Lamb Roast Florentine

> 1 pkg. (10 oz.) frozen
>   chopped spinach, thawed
>   and thoroughly drained
> 1/3 cup chopped green onion
> 2 cloves garlic, minced
> 1/2 teaspoon salt
> 1/2 teaspoon ground oregano
> 1/8 teaspoon pepper
> 4 lb. boneless rolled lamb
>   shoulder roast
>   Lemon pepper seasoning

In medium mixing bowl, combine spinach, onion, garlic, salt, oregano and pepper. Mix well.

Unroll roast. Spread with spinach mixture, leaving a 1-inch border. Roll up tightly and tie with string. Rub with lemon pepper seasoning.

Remove cooking grid. Center drip pan directly on lava rocks. Skewer and balance roast on spit. Rotiss at MEDIUM with hood closed until internal temperature reaches 160°F, 1½ to 2 hours. Let stand for 10 minutes before slicing.

6 to 8 servings

◑Elegant Oriental Veal▲

> 1½ to 1¾ lbs. veal round   1/2 cup teriyaki sauce
>   steak, 3/4 inch thick   1/2 cup dry white wine

Place veal in shallow glass baking dish or large plastic food storage bag. Pour teriyaki sauce and wine over veal. Cover dish or close bag. Refrigerate for 3 to 4 hours, turning veal over once.

Season cooking grid with vegetable oil. Preheat grill for 10 minutes. Grill veal at MEDIUM with hood closed until steaks feel slightly firm,* 15 to 18 minutes, turning over once.   *4 to 6 servings*

*Touch test, page 27.

◑Herbed Lamb Chops

> 2 tablespoons lemon juice   8 lamb loin chops, 1 to 1¼
> 1/4 teaspoon dried rosemary   inches thick
>   leaves, crushed   1 recipe Rosemary Lemon
> 1/8 teaspoon ground oregano   Butter, page 64

In small bowl, mix lemon juice, rosemary and oregano. Brush on both sides of chops, reserving remaining mixture. Let chops stand for 10 minutes. Meanwhile, prepare Rosemary Lemon Butter as directed. Set aside.

Preheat grill for 10 minutes. Brush chops with lemon mixture. Grill at MEDIUM with hood closed until chops feel slightly firm,* 10 to 15 minutes, brushing with lemon mixture and turning over frequently. Serve with Rosemary Lemon Butter.   *4 servings*

TIP: For a reduced-calorie dish, serve this recipe without the Rosemary Lemon Butter.

*Touch test, page 27.

Sausage

Grilling brings out the great smoky flavor of sausages. Both types of sausage, bulk and link, are delicious on the grill. Try bulk sausage in a casserole for a spicy main dish. Link sausage is best grilled right on the cooking grid.

You can buy sausage prepared several ways: fresh, precooked, smoked or dried.

Grill different shapes and varieties of link sausage for an interesting meal. Entertain a crowd with some quick-to-fix precooked sausages. Or add new flavor to breakfast with sausage links and patties. Use the recipes and charts on the following pages as your guide.

(1) Fresh link sausage is uncooked. Cook it thoroughly before serving. **(2) Precooked sausages**, like wieners, have been cured and fully cooked during processing. Heat them through and serve. **(3) Smoked sausages**, such as Polish sausages, may be uncooked or cooked. Check the label before grilling. **(4) Dry or semi-dry sausages,** like salami or summer sausage, are ready-to-eat. Slice and serve them warm on a toasted bun.

Hot Hero Sandwich ▲

1 loaf French bread, about
   24 inches long
¼ cup butter or margarine,
   melted
⅓ cup Thousand Island
   dressing
½ small onion, thinly
   sliced, separated into
   rings

1 green pepper, thinly sliced
   into rings
4 oz. salami, thinly sliced
4 oz. bologna, thinly sliced
2 oz. cooked turkey breast,
   thinly sliced
1 cup alfalfa sprouts
1 pkg. (8 oz.) natural
   cheese slices (Swiss,
   Colby or Cheddar)

Preheat grill for 10 minutes. Slice bread in half lengthwise. Brush
cut sides with butter. Grill, cut-side down, at MEDIUM with hood
open until bread is toasted, 1 to 2 minutes. Remove from grill.
Reduce heat to LOW.

Spread one half of bread with dressing. Layer with remaining ingredients. Top with other half of bread. Wrap in 30 × 18-inch sheet of
heavy-duty aluminum foil. Grill at LOW with hood closed until
cheese melts and sandwich is heated through, 8 to 12 minutes.

4 to 6 servings

Relish-Stuffed Franks

3 tablespoons sweet pickle
   relish
2 teaspoons prepared
   mustard
10 wieners (about 1 lb.)
5 slices bacon, cut in half
   crosswise
10 hot dog buns

Preheat grill for 10 minutes. In
small bowl, mix relish and mustard. Slit wieners lengthwise,
cutting to within ¼ inch of bottom edge. Spread about 1 teaspoon relish mixture in each
slit. Wrap one bacon half
around middle of each wiener.
Secure with wooden picks. Grill
wieners at MEDIUM with hood
closed until bacon is brown, 5
to 10 minutes, turning wieners
over and rearranging once.
Serve in buns.   *10 franks*

◄Ring Bologna with German Potato Salad

  5 slices bacon, chopped
 ½ cup chopped onion
  2 tablespoons all-purpose
     flour
  4 teaspoons sugar
  1 teaspoon salt
 ¾ teaspoon celery seed
 ¼ teaspoon pepper
  1 cup water
 ⅓ cup cider vinegar
  2 teaspoons Dijon mustard
  2 lbs. red potatoes, boiled,
     page 77
  1 ring bologna (about 1 lb.)

In 2-quart grill-safe casserole, combine bacon and onion. Remove cooking grid. Place casserole directly on lava rock grate, arranging rocks around dish.* Cook at MEDIUM-HIGH with hood open until bacon is brown and onion is tender, stirring frequently. Stir in flour, sugar, salt, celery seed and pepper. Add water, vinegar and mustard. Cook and stir with hood open until mixture is bubbly, 5 to 7 minutes. Remove from grill and set aside.

Spread lava rocks evenly across grate with long-handled tongs. Replace cooking grid. Close hood and heat grill at HIGH for 10 minutes. Slice potatoes. Stir into sauce. Cover. Place casserole on cooking grid. Score bologna at 1-inch intervals and place beside casserole on grid. Cook at HIGH with hood closed for 5 to 6 minutes, turning bologna over once. Reduce heat to MEDIUM. Place bologna in casserole on potato mixture. Re-cover. Bake using indirect MEDIUM heat with hood closed until sauce is bubbly, 20 to 30 minutes.   *4 to 6 servings*

*If your grill has two burners, cook over one burner only.

Spaghetti Sauce ▶

1 lb. bulk Italian sausage
1 lb. ground beef
¾ cup chopped onion
1 clove garlic, minced
1 can (28 oz.) whole
    tomatoes, undrained,
    cut up
1 can (16 oz.) whole
    tomatoes, undrained,
    cut up
1 can (16 oz.) tomato sauce
1 cup sliced fresh
    mushrooms
½ cup Burgundy wine
1 can (6 oz.) tomato paste
¼ cup sliced pimiento-stuffed
    olives
2 to 3 teaspoons Italian
    seasoning
2 teaspoons sugar
2 bay leaves
⅛ teaspoon ground nutmeg
    Hot cooked spaghetti

In 5-quart grill-safe casserole, combine sausage, ground beef, onion and garlic. Remove cooking grid. Place casserole directly on lava rock grate, arranging rocks around dish.* Cook at MEDIUM-HIGH with hood open until meat is no longer pink, about 10 minutes, stirring occasionally. Drain. Stir in remaining ingredients except spaghetti. Reduce heat to LOW. Simmer with hood closed until flavors are blended, 45 to 60 minutes, stirring once. Serve over spaghetti.   *6 to 8 servings*

*If your grill has two burners, cook over one burner only.

Deep Dish Skillet Pizza

pictured on page 24

- 1 loaf frozen white bread dough, thawed
- 12 oz. bulk pork sausage, browned and drained
- 1 can (4 oz.) mushroom stems and pieces, drained
- 2 tablespoons chopped onion
- 1 can (16 oz.) whole tomatoes, drained, cut up
- 1 can (8 oz.) tomato sauce
- ¾ teaspoon dried basil leaves
- ½ teaspoon sugar
- ¼ teaspoon ground oregano
- ⅛ teaspoon garlic powder
- ⅛ teaspoon dried crushed red pepper
  Pepper
- 2 cups shredded mozzarella cheese (about 8 oz.)
- ⅓ cup grated Parmesan cheese

Grease 12-inch cast-iron skillet or grill-safe baking dish. Spread bread dough evenly in bottom and slightly up sides of skillet. Sprinkle with cooked sausage, mushrooms and onion.

Preheat grill for 10 minutes. In small mixing bowl, combine tomatoes, tomato sauce, basil, sugar, oregano, garlic powder, red pepper and pepper. Spread on pizza. Top with mozzarella and Parmesan cheese.

Bake using indirect MEDIUM-HIGH heat with hood closed until crust is deep golden brown, 40 to 50 minutes. Let pizza stand for 10 minutes before cutting.   *4 servings*

Hearty Sausage Stew▲

- 1½ to 2 lbs. fully-cooked sausage (bratwurst, bologna or Polish sausage)
- 2 cans (16 oz. each) great northern beans, undrained
- 3 cups coarsely-chopped cabbage
- 2 cups water
- 1½ cups sliced carrots, 1-inch pieces
- 1 can (10¾ oz.) condensed chicken broth
- ¾ cup sliced celery, ½-inch pieces
- 1 tablespoon instant minced onion
- ½ teaspoon dried basil leaves
- ¼ teaspoon dried thyme leaves
- ¼ teaspoon dried summer savory leaves
- ⅛ teaspoon instant minced garlic

Cut sausage into 1½-inch pieces. Place in 5-quart grill-safe casserole. Stir in remaining ingredients. Cover.

Remove cooking grid. Place casserole directly on lava rock grate, arranging rocks around dish.* Cook at HIGH with hood open until mixture boils. Reduce heat to LOW. Simmer with hood closed until carrots are tender, 30 to 35 minutes, stirring once.   *6 to 8 servings*

*If your grill has two burners, cook over one burner only.

Sausage-Stuffed Peppers

4 medium green peppers
12 oz. bulk pork sausage
⅓ cup chopped onion
⅓ cup chopped celery
3 cups cooked white rice
1 cup salsa
1 to 2 tablespoons chopped
   canned green chilies
1 teaspoon instant chicken
   bouillon granules
2 cups shredded Monterey
   Jack cheese (about 8 oz.)
¼ cup salsa

4 to 6 servings

How to Make Sausage-Stuffed Peppers

Cut peppers in half lengthwise. Remove seeds and stems. Set aside. Preheat grill for 10 minutes. If your grill has two burners, preheat one burner only.

Combine sausage, onion and celery in cast-iron skillet or grill-safe baking dish. Place skillet on cooking grid.

Cook and stir until sausage is no longer pink and onion is tender-crisp, 5 to 10 minutes. Drain. Stir in rice, 1 cup salsa, chilies and bouillon granules.

Fill peppers with sausage mixture. Arrange in skillet. Top with cheese and ¼ cup salsa. Cover tightly.

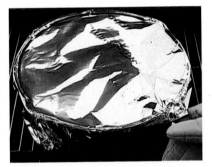

Bake using indirect MEDIUM heat with hood closed until peppers are tender, 45 to 55 minutes, rotating skillet once.

Sausage Cooking Guide

ITEM	HEAT SETTING	COOKING TIME	METHOD
Sausage Links (fully cooked) 3 to 4 oz. each	HIGH	5 to 7 min.	Preheat grill for 10 minutes. Score sausages in 2 or 3 places. Grill with hood open. Turn sausages several times.
Sausage Links (uncooked) 3 to 4 oz. each	MEDIUM	15 to 20 min.	Preheat grill for 10 minutes. Grill with hood closed. Turn sausages over and rearrange several times.
Sausage Patties (uncooked) 2 oz. each ½ inch thick	MEDIUM	5 to 7 min.	Preheat grill for 5 minutes.* Place seasoned griddle on cooking grid. Preheat for 5 minutes longer. Place sausages on griddle. Grill with hood open. Turn patties over once.
Wieners	HIGH	3 to 5 min.	Preheat grill for 10 minutes. Grill with hood open. Turn wieners several times.

If your grill has two burners, preheat and cook over one burner only.

Poultry

Poultry is popular any way you grill it. Fix it simply for the family or elegantly for guests. Bake it in a casserole or cook it on the rotisserie. Poultry is versatile, economical and nutritious.

Use the low or medium heat setting to cook poultry thoroughly without burning. The gas grill makes it easy to regulate the cooking temperature.

Grill poultry with the skin on to keep the meat moist and flavorful. Flare-ups may occur when fat from the skin drips onto the lava rocks. To prevent burning, rearrange poultry pieces frequently or place a drip pan on the lava rocks under whole poultry. For a reduced-calorie main dish, grill poultry with the skin removed. Season the cooking grid before grilling to keep the pieces from sticking.

◀Orange-Glazed Cornish Hens

⅔ cup orange marmalade
1 teaspoon dried tarragon leaves
¾ teaspoon onion salt
4 Cornish hens (about 24 oz. each), thawed, giblets removed

In small bowl, combine marmalade, tarragon and onion salt. Mix well. Set aside.

Remove cooking grid. Center drip pan directly on lava rocks. Skewer and balance hens lengthwise on spit. With string, tie legs and wings close to body of each hen. Rotiss hens at MEDIUM with hood closed until internal temperature reaches 185°F, about 1 hour. Brush with glaze during last 15 minutes. Brush again before serving.

4 servings

❶ Herbed Chicken with Vegetables

3 stalks celery, cut into
  1-inch pieces
8 oz. whole fresh
  mushrooms
1 medium tomato, cut into
  8 pieces
1 tablespoon butter or
  margarine, cut up
¼ teaspoon salt
¼ teaspoon dried basil or
  marjoram leaves
⅛ teaspoon pepper
2 chicken breasts, split in
  half
  Seasoned salt

Preheat grill for 10 minutes. In
8-inch square grill-safe baking
dish, combine celery, mushrooms, tomato, butter, salt,
basil and pepper. Stir. Place
dish on cooking grid. Arrange
chicken, bone-side down, on
cooking grid beside vegetables.
Sprinkle chicken with seasoned
salt. Grill at MEDIUM with
hood closed for 5 minutes.

Turn chicken over and sprinkle
with seasoned salt. Stir vegetables. Grill with hood closed for
5 minutes longer. Arrange
chicken on vegetables. Cover.
Bake using indirect MEDIUM
heat with hood closed until
meat near bone is no longer
pink, about 40 minutes.

4 servings

TIP: For a reduced-calorie
dish, remove chicken skin before grilling. Season cooking
grid with vegetable cooking
spray before preheating grill.
Substitute lemon or apple juice
for butter.

Chicken Chow Mein Casserole

2 cups diagonally-sliced
 celery, 1/4-inch pieces
1 cup chopped onion
1/3 cup chopped carrot
3 tablespoons vegetable oil
2 cups cut-up cooked
 chicken
1 can (10 3/4 oz.) condensed
 cream of chicken soup
1 can (8 oz.) sliced water
 chestnuts, drained
3/4 cup water
1 can (4 oz.) sliced
 mushrooms, drained
1 jar (2 oz.) sliced
 pimiento, drained
2 tablespoons soy sauce
1/4 teaspoon pepper
 Chow mein noodles

In 3-quart grill-safe casserole, combine celery, onion, carrot and oil. Remove cooking grid. Place casserole directly on lava rock grate, arranging rocks around dish.* Cook and stir at MEDIUM-HIGH until vegetables are tender-crisp, about 15 minutes. Remove from heat. Stir in remaining ingredients except chow mein noodles. Cover and set aside.

Spread lava rocks evenly across grate with long-handled tongs. Replace cooking grid. Close hood and heat grill at HIGH for 10 minutes. Bake casserole using indirect MEDIUM heat with hood closed until hot and bubbly, 25 to 30 minutes. Serve over chow mein noodles.

4 to 6 servings

*If your grill has two burners, cook over one burner only.

Sweet-and-Spicy Chicken

1/2 cup apricot preserves
1/4 cup French dressing
2 tablespoons finely-chopped
 onion
2 tablespoons lemon juice
1 tablespoon packed brown
 sugar
1/4 teaspoon pepper
2 broiler-fryer chickens
 (about 2 1/2 lbs. each),
 cut up

Preheat grill for 10 minutes. In small bowl, blend all ingredients except chicken. Set aside.

Grill chicken at LOW with hood closed until meat near bone is no longer pink, 35 to 45 minutes, turning pieces over and rearranging frequently. Brush with sauce during last 15 to 20 minutes of grilling.

6 to 8 servings

Lemon Chicken ▲

1/3 cup lemon juice
2 tablespoons vegetable oil
1 teaspoon Worcestershire
 sauce
3/4 teaspoon onion salt
1/2 teaspoon dried thyme
 leaves
1/2 teaspoon pepper
1 clove garlic, minced
1 broiler-fryer chicken
 (about 2 1/2 lbs.),
 quartered

Preheat grill for 10 minutes. In small bowl, blend all ingredients except chicken. Set aside.

Tuck wing tips under cut side of chicken. Grill chicken at LOW with hood closed until meat near bone is no longer pink, 35 to 45 minutes, turning chicken over and rearranging frequently. Brush with sauce during last 15 to 20 minutes of grilling.

2 to 4 servings

53

Mexican Chicken Bake

2 cups cut-up cooked chicken
1 can (8 oz.) whole tomatoes, undrained, cut up
2 tablespoons chopped onion
1 tablespoon canned chopped green chilies
½ teaspoon ground cumin

1 cup dairy sour cream
¾ cup shredded Cheddar cheese (about 3 oz.)
1 cup shredded Monterey Jack cheese (about 4 oz.)
1 egg
2½ cups corn chips
¼ cup shredded Cheddar cheese (about 1 oz.)

In small mixing bowl, combine chicken, tomatoes, onion, chilies and cumin. Mix well. Set aside. In small mixing bowl, blend sour cream, ¾ cup Cheddar cheese, Monterey Jack cheese and egg.

Preheat grill for 10 minutes. Grease 2-quart grill-safe casserole. Spread half the corn chips in dish. Layer with half the chicken mixture and half the sour cream mixture. Repeat chicken and sour cream layers. Top with remaining corn chips and ¼ cup Cheddar cheese. Bake using indirect MEDIUM heat with hood closed until heated through, about 1 hour.

4 to 6 servings

Poultry Cooking Guide

ITEM	HEAT SETTING	COOKING TIME	METHOD
Chicken Pieces 2½ to 5 lbs. 4 to 8 servings	LOW	35 to 45 min.	Preheat grill for 10 minutes. Grill chicken until juices run clear, turning over several times. Brush with sauce during last 15 minutes, if desired.
●Whole Chicken (broiler-fryer) 2½ to 3 lbs. 3 to 4 servings	MEDIUM	1 to 1½ hrs.	Remove cooking grid. Center drip pan on lava rocks. Skewer and balance chicken on spit. With string, tie legs and wings close to body. Rotiss until internal temperature of chicken reaches 185°F. Let stand for 10 minutes before carving.
Whole Duckling 4½ to 5 lbs. 3 to 4 servings	MEDIUM	1½ to 2½ hrs.	Remove cooking grid. Center drip pan on lava rocks. Skewer and balance duckling on spit. With string, tie legs and wings close to body. Rotiss until internal temperature of duckling reaches 185°F. Let stand for 10 minutes before carving.
●Whole Turkey 9 to 10 lbs. 8 to 10 servings	MEDIUM	3 to 4 hrs.	Remove cooking grid. Place drip pan filled with 1 to 2 inches water directly on lava rocks on one half of grate. Replace cooking grid. Preheat grill for 10 minutes. Place turkey, breast-side up, on grid above drip pan. Roast using indirect heat with hood closed until internal temperature of turkey reaches 185°F, rotating turkey once. Let stand for 10 minutes before carving.

54

Smoked Stuffed Turkey

4 cups crushed herb-seasoned
   stuffing mix
⅔ cup chopped onion
½ cup thinly-sliced celery
½ cup chopped walnuts
½ cup raisins
2 teaspoons instant chicken
   bouillon granules
1 cup boiling water
½ cup butter or margarine,
   melted
1 jar (9 oz.) chutney
¼ cup brandy or apple juice
9 to 10 lb. whole turkey,
   thawed, giblets removed
2 lbs. wood chips, soaked,
   pages 12, 13

8 to 10 servings

How to Make Smoked Stuffed Turkey

Mix stuffing mix, onion, celery, walnuts, raisins and bouillon granules in large mixing bowl. Stir in water and butter. In small mixing bowl, mix chutney and brandy. Stir into stuffing mixture. Stuff loosely into turkey cavity. Wrap wood chips in heavy-duty aluminum foil to make logs (pages 12, 13). Remove cooking grid.

Move lava rocks onto one half of grate. Place one foil log on lava rocks. Preheat grill for 10 minutes.

Place shallow drip pan filled with 1 to 2 inches water on empty half of lava rock grate. Replace cooking grid over drip pan. Close hood.

After wood chips ignite (10 to 20 minutes), place turkey on cooking grid over drip pan. Roast turkey using indirect MEDIUM heat with hood closed until internal temperature reaches 185°F, 3 to 4 hours, rotating turkey once. Replace foil logs as needed for continuous smoking. Let turkey stand for 10 minutes before carving.

Fish & Seafood

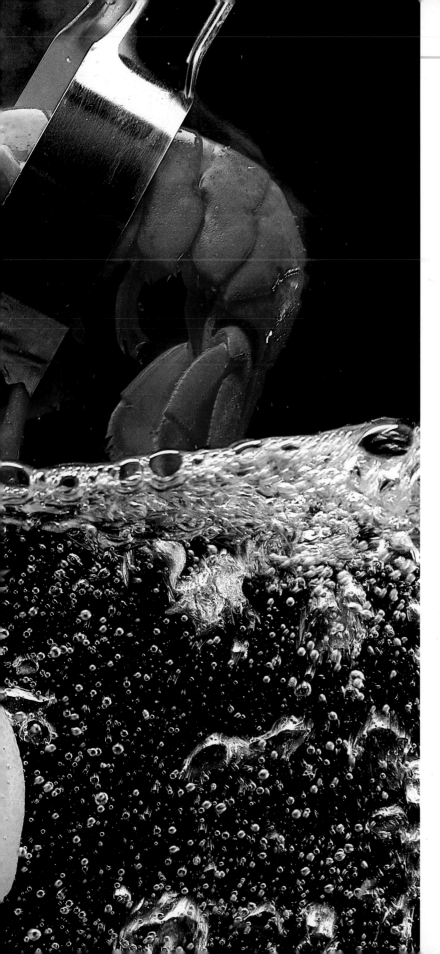

Grilling enhances the mild taste of seafood. A great variety of fish and shellfish is available at most supermarkets. Take advantage of this selection for new flavors from your grill.

Seafood is popular frozen or canned, but fresh is by far the best. Buy fresh fish and shellfish that are firm and have a mild, fresh odor. Frozen seafood should be solid and tightly packaged. Defrost it for about 24 hours in the refrigerator before cooking.

Cook seafood quickly yet thoroughly. Overcooking makes it dry and tough, with poor flavor. Fish is thoroughly cooked when it becomes opaque and flakes easily with a fork. Shellfish should be opaque and firm.

Grill fish directly on a lightly seasoned cooking grid or in a flat grill basket. The basket makes turning easy and keeps fish from falling apart. Combine shrimp and scallops for grilled seafood kabobs. Use shellfish of similar size for even cooking. Boil live lobster on your gas grill and drizzle it with a special butter or spicy sauce. Any way you serve it, you'll love what the gas grill does for the flavor of seafood.

Boiled Lobster, page 58

57

Boiled Lobster

4 quarts hot water
6 to 8 slices lemon
4 to 6 peppercorns
2 tablespoons salt

Sauce:

½ cup clarified butter
1 tablespoon lemon juice
1 teaspoon dried parsley
   flakes
¼ teaspoon garlic powder

2 live lobsters (about 1 lb.
   each)

2 servings

How to Make Boiled Lobster

Combine water, lemon slices, peppercorns and salt in 6-quart grill-safe saucepan. Remove cooking grid. Cover saucepan. If your grill has two burners, cook over one burner only.

Place saucepan directly on lava rock grate. Arrange rocks around saucepan with long-handled tongs.

Cook at HIGH with hood open until water boils. Meanwhile, in small grill-safe bowl, mix sauce ingredients. Set aside.

Place lobsters, head first, into water. Re-cover. Cook with hood closed until mixture boils. Reduce heat to LOW.

Simmer with hood closed for 12 to 15 minutes. Place sauce on edge of upper cooking rack during last 2 to 3 minutes of cooking.

Drain lobsters and rinse in cold water. Split and clean lobsters. Serve with sauce.

◗Seafood Kabobs

1 recipe Seasoned Butter
   Baste, page 64
1 large green pepper, cut
   into 16 pieces
1 medium onion, quartered
   and separated into pieces
4 medium carrots, cut into
   1½-inch pieces
16 sea scallops (about 1 lb.)
24 large or jumbo shrimp
   (about 1 lb.), shelled and
   deveined

4 kabobs

Prepare baste as directed. Set
aside. Parboil green pepper,
onion and carrots until tender-
crisp, 10 to 12 minutes. Rinse
in cold water. Set aside. Season
cooking grid with vegetable oil.
Preheat grill for 10 minutes.

Alternate vegetables, scallops
and shrimp on four 16 to 18-
inch skewers. Place kabobs on
cooking grid. Brush with baste.
Grill at MEDIUM with hood
closed until seafood is opaque
and firm, 15 to 18 minutes,
turning over and brushing with
baste several times.

Seafood Rice ▲

1 cup long grain white rice,
   uncooked
¼ cup chopped green pepper
¼ cup chopped onion
1 teaspoon salt
2 cups water
1 pkg. (6 oz.) frozen cooked
   crab meat and shrimp,
   thawed
1 tablespoon snipped fresh
   parsley
1 cup picante sauce

In 3-quart grill-safe casserole, combine rice, green pepper, onion
and salt. Stir in water. Cover. Remove cooking grid. Place casserole directly on lava rock grate, arranging rocks around dish.* Cook
at HIGH with hood open until mixture boils. Stir. Re-cover. Reduce
heat to LOW. Cook with hood closed until water is absorbed, about
15 minutes. Stir in seafood, parsley and picante sauce. Cook and
stir with hood open until heated through, 1 to 2 minutes.   *6 servings*

*If your grill has two burners, cook over one burner only.

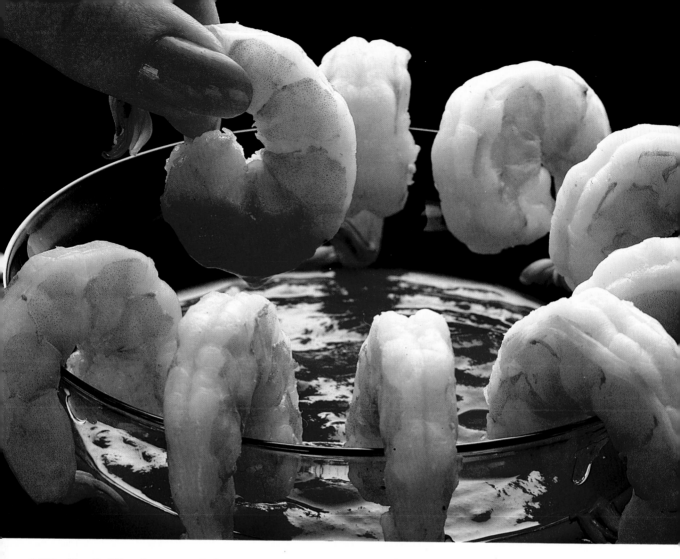

❶Boiled Shrimp with Seafood Sauce ▲

1/2 cup chili sauce
1/2 cup ketchup
1 tablespoon lemon juice
6 cups water
2 tablespoons pickling spice
1 lb. large or jumbo shrimp, shelled and deveined

In small mixing bowl, mix chili sauce, ketchup and lemon juice. Set aside.

Place water in 3-quart grill-safe casserole. Tie pickling spice in small piece of cheesecloth. Place in water. Cover. Remove cooking grid. Place casserole directly on lava rock grate, arranging rocks around dish.* Cook at HIGH with hood open until water boils. Boil for 10 minutes. Add shrimp. Reduce heat to MEDIUM. Cook until shrimp are opaque and firm, 5 to 8 minutes, stirring occasionally. Remove from heat. Drain shrimp. Serve warm or cold with sauce.   *4 servings*

*If your grill has two burners, cook over one burner only.

Shrimp Scampi

1/2 cup butter or margarine
2 tablespoons olive oil
3 cloves garlic, minced
1 lb. large or jumbo shrimp, shelled and deveined
2 tablespoons snipped fresh parsley
2 tablespoons dry white wine
1 tablespoon lemon juice
Salt and pepper
Hot cooked rice

In 2½-quart grill-safe casserole, combine butter, oil and garlic. Remove cooking grid. Place casserole directly on lava rock grate, arranging rocks around dish.* Cook at HIGH with hood open until butter melts. Add shrimp. Cook and stir until shrimp are opaque and firm, 5 to 8 minutes. Remove shrimp from butter. Stir in remaining ingredients except rice. Cook and stir at HIGH for 1 minute. Stir in shrimp. Serve with rice.
        4 servings

*If your grill has two burners, cook over one burner only.

Fillets with Seafood Rice Stuffing ▶

1 recipe Seafood Rice,
   page 59
4 red snapper, sole, orange
   roughy, or flounder fillets
   (about 1½ lbs.)
4 slices lemon

Prepare Seafood Rice as directed. Remove 2 cups mixture. Cover remaining mixture to keep it warm. Set aside.

Preheat grill for 10 minutes.

Spread ½ cup Seafood Rice down center of each fillet. Roll up fillets. Secure seams with wooden picks.

Place each roll, seam-side down, on one lemon slice in 8-inch square grill-safe baking dish or on 24 × 18-inch sheet of heavy-duty aluminum foil. Cover pan or bundle wrap foil (page 14). Bake using indirect MEDIUM heat with hood closed until fish flakes easily with fork, 40 to 50 minutes. Serve with remaining Seafood Rice.

4 servings

Seasonings, Sauces &
Marinades

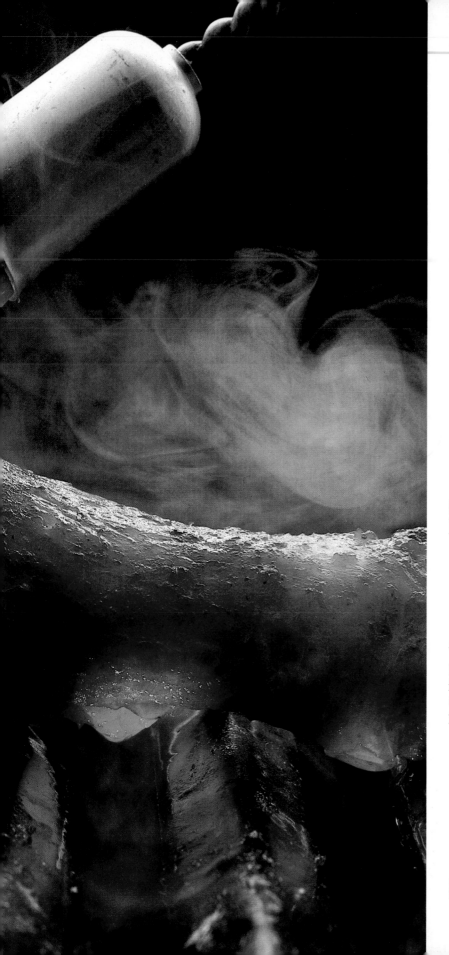

Make an ordinary burger or cut of meat into a zesty main dish. Turn an inexpensive steak or roast into one that's tender and juicy. With a simple sauce or marinade, you can make your grilled meats, poultry and seafood extra special.

Spice up basic burgers and plain meats with one of the seasoning mixtures below. Store leftover seasoning in a handy shaker for your next cookout.

Seasoning for Beef

> 1 tablespoon paprika
> 1 tablespoon garlic salt
> 1 tablespoon onion powder
> 1½ teaspoons pepper

In small bowl, combine all ingredients. Before grilling, sprinkle lightly onto steaks, roasts or hamburgers. Store in cool, dry place.   *About ¼ cup*

Seasoning for Poultry or Pork

> 3 tablespoons paprika
> 1 tablespoon celery salt
> 2 teaspoons ground
>   coriander
> 1 teaspoon chili powder
> 1 teaspoon cayenne
> ½ teaspoon ground nutmeg

In small bowl, combine all ingredients. Before grilling, sprinkle lightly onto poultry or pork. Store in cool, dry place.
    About ¼ cup

Chicken Pieces (page 54) with Easy Barbecue Sauce (page 64)

Sauces & Bastes

Sauces and bastes which are high in sugar burn easily, so apply them during the last 10 to 20 minutes of grilling. Use a long-handled basting brush with soft bristles to thoroughly coat the meat, poultry or seafood.

Seasoned Butter Baste

¼ cup butter or margarine, softened
½ teaspoon paprika
¼ teaspoon onion salt
* 1 clove garlic, minced*

In grill-safe custard cup, blend all ingredients. Place on edge of cooking grid or upper cooking rack. Remove from grill when butter melts. Brush on meats, seafood, fish or vegetables during grilling.

Rosemary Lemon Butter (for poultry and lamb): Follow recipe above, omitting paprika. Add 1 teaspoon dried rosemary leaves and ½ teaspoon grated lemon peel. Brush on poultry or lamb during grilling.

Dill Lemon Butter (for fish and seafood): Follow recipe above, omitting paprika. Add ½ teaspoon dried dill weed and ½ teaspoon grated lemon peel. Brush on fish or seafood during grilling.

About ¼ cup

Easy Barbecue Sauce ▲

½ cup ketchup
2 tablespoons cider vinegar
2 tablespoons maple syrup
2 tablespoons grated onion
2 teaspoons prepared mustard
½ teaspoon ground thyme
¼ teaspoon cayenne

In small mixing bowl, blend all ingredients. Brush on meat or poultry during last 10 to 20 minutes of grilling. *About 1 cup*

Teriyaki Sauce

½ cup soy sauce
⅓ cup vegetable oil
2 tablespoons light corn syrup
2 tablespoons white wine vinegar
2 cloves garlic, minced
1 teaspoon ground ginger
1 teaspoon dry mustard

In small mixing bowl, blend all ingredients. Pour over beef, poultry or shrimp. Cover dish or close bag. Refrigerate for at least 8 hours. *About 1 cup*

Spicy Barbecue Sauce

2 cans (15 oz. each) tomato sauce
1 can (16 oz.) whole tomatoes, undrained
1 can (6 oz.) tomato paste
1 medium onion, chopped
1 medium cooking apple, peeled and chopped
¾ cup packed brown sugar
⅔ cup vinegar
½ cup chopped celery
¼ cup molasses
2 slices lemon
2 tablespoons chili powder
2 tablespoons vegetable oil
1 tablespoon dry mustard
1 tablespoon Worcestershire sauce
1 stick cinnamon
2 cloves garlic, cut in half
8 whole peppercorns
½ teaspoon pepper

In grill-safe Dutch oven, combine all ingredients. Stir to blend and break apart tomatoes. Remove cooking grid. Place pan on lava rock grate, arranging rocks around pan.* Cook and stir at HIGH with hood open until mixture boils. Reduce heat to LOW. Simmer until sauce is desired consistency, 1 to 1½ hours. Cool slightly. Strain. Brush on meat or poultry during last 10 to 20 minutes of grilling. *5 to 5½ cups*

*If your grill has two burners, cook over one burner only.

Marinades

Marinating tenderizes tough meat fibers in less-tender cuts. Before grilling, place meat in a glass dish or large plastic food storage bag and pour marinade over the meat. A plastic bag is ideal because it keeps the marinade in contact with the meat. Marinate for at least 8 hours in the refrigerator, turning meat over occasionally.

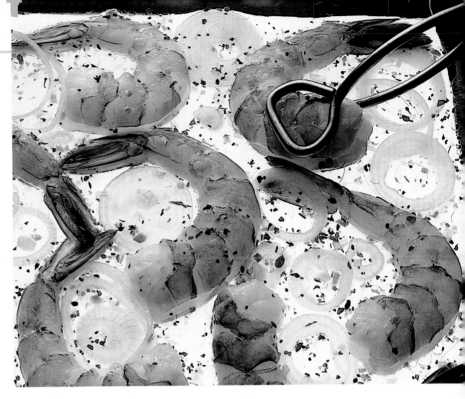

Orange Spice Marinade

    1 can (6 oz.) frozen orange
        juice concentrate, thawed
    1/4 cup water
    2 tablespoons vinegar
    1 tablespoon vegetable oil
    2 bay leaves
    1/2 teaspoon ground allspice
    1/4 teaspoon onion powder

In small grill-safe saucepan, combine all ingredients. Remove cooking grid. Place pan on lava rock grate, arranging rocks around pan.* Cook at HIGH with hood open until mixture boils. Reduce heat to LOW. Simmer for 1 minute, stirring constantly. Remove from heat; cool slightly. Pour over poultry, beef or lamb. Cover dish or close bag. Refrigerate for at least 8 hours.

1¼ cups

*If your grill has two burners, cook over one burner only.

Italian Marinade

    1 cup Italian dressing
    1 small onion, thinly sliced
    1/8 teaspoon pepper

In small bowl, mix all ingredients. Pour over poultry, shrimp or less tender cuts of beef. Cover dish or close bag. Refrigerate for at least 8 hours. *1 cup*

Lemon Marinade

    1 can (6 oz.) frozen
        lemonade concentrate,
        thawed
    2 tablespoons vegetable oil
    1 tablespoon Worcestershire
        sauce
    1 teaspoon dry mustard

In small mixing bowl, blend all ingredients. Pour over poultry, lamb or ribs. Cover dish or close bag. Refrigerate for at least 8 hours. *About 1 cup*

Tomato Beer Marinade

    1 bottle (7 oz.) beer
    1 cup tomato juice
    1 small onion, sliced
    1 tablespoon packed brown
        sugar
    1/4 teaspoon celery salt
    1/8 teaspoon garlic powder
    6 to 8 drops hot pepper
        sauce

In small mixing bowl, blend all ingredients. Pour over beef chuck or pot roast. Cover dish or close bag. Refrigerate for at least 8 hours. *About 2 cups*

Pineapple Curry Marinade

    1 can (6 oz.) frozen
        pineapple juice
        concentrate, thawed
    1/3 cup chopped green
        pepper
    1/3 cup coarsely-chopped
        green onion
    1/4 cup soy sauce
    1½ teaspoons curry powder

In small grill-safe saucepan, combine all ingredients. Remove cooking grid. Place saucepan directly on lava rock grate, arranging rocks around pan.* Cook at HIGH with hood open until mixture boils. Reduce heat to LOW. Simmer for 1 minute, stirring constantly. Remove from heat and cool slightly. Pour over beef, lamb, pork or poultry. Cover dish or close bag. Refrigerate for at least 8 hours.

About 1 cup

*If your grill has two burners cook over one burner only.

Eggs & Cheese

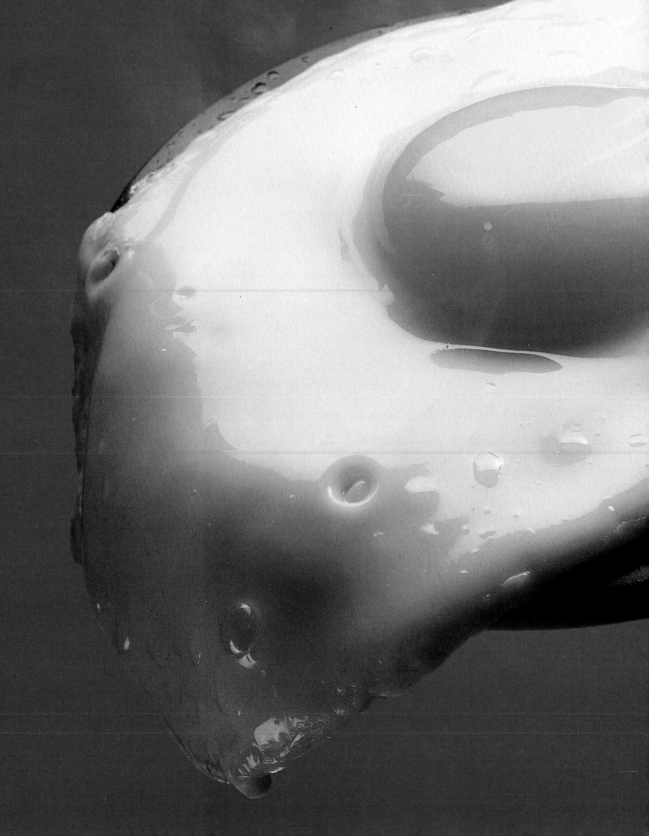

Eggs and cheese are a delicious, economical way to enjoy a meatless main dish. Serve them at breakfast, brunch, lunch or dinner as a nutritious part of your meal.

Try something new with eggs and cheese — prepare them on the gas grill. The versatile gas grill is ideal for everything from simple fried eggs to unique Potted Peppers (page 68).

Breakfast Sandwiches

¼ cup mayonnaise
1 teaspoon prepared mustard
4 eggs
4 slices Canadian bacon
4 English muffins, split and
    toasted
4 slices Cheddar cheese
    (¾ oz. each)

In small bowl, mix mayonnaise and mustard. Set aside. Preheat grill for 5 minutes.* Generously season egg rings or 3½-inch screw bands from canning jars. Season griddle or skillet. Place griddle on one half of cooking grid. Arrange egg rings on one half of griddle. Preheat grill for 5 minutes longer. Break one egg into each ring. Grill at HIGH with hood open until yolks are slightly set, about 3 minutes.

Arrange bacon on other half of griddle. Grill with hood open 1 to 2 minutes, turning over once.

Spread each English muffin half with mayonnaise mixture. Place 1 egg on each of 4 muffin halves. Layer with bacon and cheese. Top with remaining muffin halves. Place sandwiches on griddle. Grill with hood closed until cheese melts, 4 to 5 minutes.   *4 servings*

*If your grill has two burners, preheat and cook over one burner only.

Fried Eggs, page 69

67

Potted Peppers ▲

4 medium green peppers
8 eggs
¼ cup vodka
8 drops hot pepper sauce
½ cup shredded process
    American cheese food
    (about 2 oz.)
    Salsa or picante sauce

Remove tops and seeds from peppers. Stand peppers upright. Break 2 eggs into each pepper. Add 1 tablespoon vodka and 2 drops hot pepper sauce to each. Top with cheese. Preheat grill for 10 minutes.* Bundle wrap each pepper (page 14). Grill at MEDIUM with hood closed until eggs are set, 25 to 30 minutes. Serve with salsa.

4 servings

*If your grill has two burners, preheat and cook over one burner only.

Deluxe Grilled Cheese Sandwiches

1 cup shredded Swiss
    cheese (about 4 oz.)
1 cup shredded Cheddar
    cheese (about 4 oz.)
⅓ cup mayonnaise
1 tablespoon prepared
    mustard
1 tablespoon finely-chopped
    green onion
8 slices bread
4 thin slices fully-cooked
    ham (optional)
¼ cup butter or margarine,
    softened

In small mixing bowl, blend Swiss cheese, Cheddar cheese, mayonnaise, mustard and onion. Divide and spread evenly on 4 slices bread. Add 1 slice ham to each. Top with remaining bread. Spread outside of sandwiches with butter.

Preheat grill for 5 minutes.* Place griddle on cooking grid. Preheat for 5 minutes longer. Place sandwiches on griddle. Grill at MEDIUM-HIGH with hood open until golden brown, 4 to 6 minutes, turning over once.

4 sandwiches

*If your grill has two burners, preheat and cook over one burner only.

Cheesy Sausage Bake

1 pkg. (8 oz.) refrigerated
   crescent rolls
12 oz. bulk pork sausage,
   browned and drained
1 cup shredded Cheddar
   cheese (about 4 oz.)
1 cup shredded Monterey
   Jack cheese (about 4 oz.)
4 eggs, slightly beaten
¾ cup milk
¼ teaspoon salt
¼ teaspoon dried basil
   leaves
⅛ teaspoon pepper

Preheat grill for 10 minutes.
Grease 9-inch square grill-safe
baking dish. Unroll crescent roll
dough. Press evenly in bottom
and 1½ inches up sides of prepared dish, cutting to fit as
needed. Spread sausage over
crust. Sprinkle with cheeses.

In small mixing bowl, blend
remaining ingredients. Pour
onto cheese. Bake using indirect MEDIUM heat with hood
closed until set, 25 to 35 minutes, rotating dish once.

6 to 8 servings

Egg Cooking Guide

ITEM	HEAT SETTING	COOKING TIME	METHOD
Fried Eggs, 4	HIGH	1 to 2 min.	Preheat grill for 5 minutes.* Place griddle on cooking grid. Preheat for 5 minutes longer. Season griddle with 1 tablespoon butter or margarine. Break 4 eggs onto griddle. Cook with hood open to desired doneness.
Scrambled Eggs, 4	HIGH	1 to 2 min.	Preheat and season griddle as directed above. In small mixing bowl, mix 4 eggs, 2 tablespoons milk, ½ teaspoon salt and ¼ teaspoon pepper. Slowly pour mixture onto griddle, pushing eggs toward center with spatula. Cook with hood open to desired doneness.

If your grill has two burners, preheat and cook over one burner only.

Fruits & Vegetables

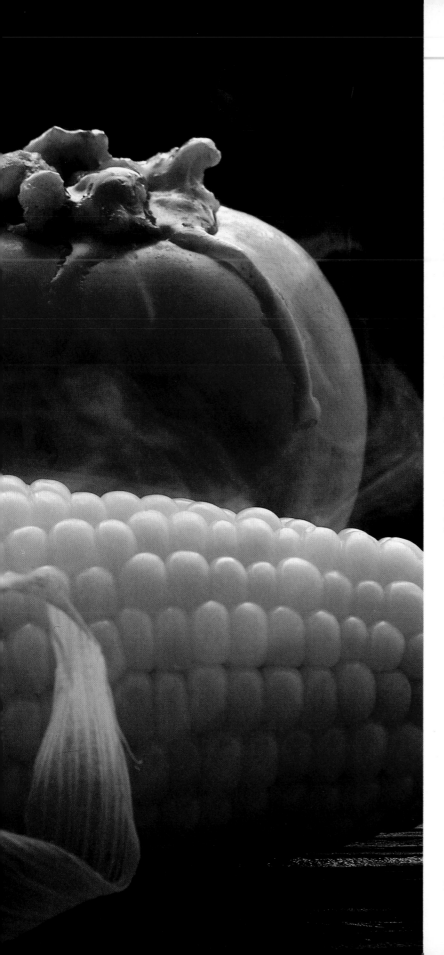

No meal is complete without the nutrition and fresh flavor of fruit and vegetables. Cooking is fast and clean-up is easy when you cook these foods on the grill. Try our recipes for everything from Dilled Carrots to Acorn Squash to Baked Apples. Cook an entire meal by preparing the fruit and vegetables on your gas grill along with the main meal.

Wrap vegetables in foil packets so there's no casserole or pan to wash. Use a drugstore wrap or bundle wrap (page 14) to seal in moisture. Add a few ice cubes to the packet before grilling. As the packet heats, the ice melts and vegetables steam to perfection.

When grilling fruit or vegetables directly on the cooking grid, season the grid with vegetable oil or vegetable cooking spray *before preheating*. Unlike most meats and poultry, vegetables and fruit have no fat to keep them from sticking.

Baked Apples, page 73
Corn on the Cob, page 77

Mixed Grilled Fruit

1 can (16 oz.) peach halves, drained
2 tablespoons brandy
2 tablespoons strawberry jelly
1 tablespoon honey
1 tablespoon butter or margarine
1 grapefruit, cut in half
1 can (8 oz.) sliced pineapple, drained
2 large firm bananas
  Toasted flaked coconut

6 servings

How to Make Mixed Grilled Fruit

Place peach halves in large shallow dish or large plastic food storage bag. Sprinkle with brandy. Let stand for 10 to 15 minutes.

Season cooking grid with vegetable oil. Preheat grill for 10 minutes. In grill-safe custard cup or small bowl, combine jelly, honey and butter.

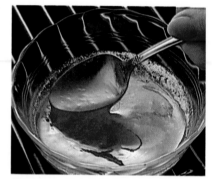

Set bowl on edge of cooking grid. Cook at MEDIUM until jelly melts, about 2 minutes, stirring occasionally. Remove from grill.

Place grapefruit halves, cut-side down, on cooking grid. Grill for 1 minute at MEDIUM with hood open.

Arrange peaches, pineapple and bananas on grid with grapefruit. Brush with glaze. Grill with hood open.

Grill until fruit is seared with grid lines, 4 to 6 minutes, turning over and brushing with glaze once. Remove from grill. Sprinkle with coconut.

Baked Apples ▶

also pictured on page 71

4 medium cooking apples	1 tablespoon maple syrup
¼ cup chopped walnuts	¼ teaspoon ground cinnamon
¼ cup packed brown sugar	

Preheat grill for 10 minutes. Core apples. Peel a thin strip of skin from around top of each apple to allow steam to escape. Place apples upright in 8-inch square grill-safe baking dish. Set aside. In small mixing bowl, combine remaining ingredients. Mix well. Press about 1 tablespoon brown sugar mixture into each apple. Cover. Bake using indirect MEDIUM heat with hood closed until apples are tender, 25 to 35 minutes.

4 servings

Hawaiian Fruit Kabobs

pictured on cover

1 fresh pineapple, cut in half lengthwise
1 can (16 oz.) apricot halves
¼ cup packed brown sugar
2 tablespoons honey
2 tablespoons rum (optional)
¼ teaspoon ground cinnamon
12 maraschino cherries
1 medium pear, cut into 12 chunks
12 large marshmallows (optional)

12 kabobs

How to Make Hawaiian Fruit Kabobs

Remove crown, stem and core of one pineapple half. Slice off rind in lengthwise strips. Cut away eyes. Cut pineapple half into twelve 2-inch wedges. Set other pineapple half aside.

Preheat grill for 10 minutes. Drain apricot halves, reserving ½ cup juice. Set apricots aside. In 13 × 9-inch grill-safe baking dish, combine apricot juice, brown sugar, honey, rum and cinnamon. Set aside.

Place 1 cherry in center of each of 12 apricot halves. Alternate pear, apricots with cherries, and pineapple on twelve 10 to 12-inch skewers. Arrange in dish with sauce. Place dish on cooking grid.

Place remaining pineapple half, cut-side down, on cooking grid. Grill at MEDIUM with hood closed until pineapple half is seared with grid lines, about 5 minutes. Turn pineapple over.

Push tip of each skewer into cut side of pineapple, standing skewers upright. Place 1 marshmallow on the end of each skewer. Grill with hood open until marshmallows are warm, about 1 minute.

Herbed Potatoes and Carrots ▲

4 small potatoes, very
  thinly sliced
1 medium onion, very
  thinly sliced
4 carrots, very thinly sliced
2 tablespoons Italian
  dressing
¼ teaspoon salt
¼ teaspoon Italian seasoning
⅛ teaspoon pepper
2 ice cubes
  Dairy sour cream
  (optional)

Preheat grill for 10 minutes.
Arrange potatoes, onions and
carrots on 24 × 18-inch double
thickness of heavy-duty aluminum foil. Sprinkle with Italian
dressing, salt, Italian seasoning
and pepper. Add ice cubes.
Drugstore wrap (page 14).

Cook at MEDIUM with hood
closed until vegetables are
tender, 20 to 25 minutes,
turning packet over once.
Serve with sour cream.

4 to 6 servings

Bacon-Wrapped Baked Potatoes

4 medium baking potatoes
  Salt and pepper
8 thin slices green pepper
  (rings)
8 thin slices onion
2 tablespoons butter or
  margarine
8 slices bacon

Preheat grill for 10 minutes.
Cut potatoes in half lengthwise.
Set aside 4 halves. Place each
remaining half, cut-side up, on a
14 × 14-inch double thickness of
heavy-duty aluminum foil.
Sprinkle with salt and pepper.
Top each with 2 green pepper
slices and 2 onion slices. Dot
with ½ tablespoon butter. Top
with remaining 4 potato halves.
On top of each potato, criss-
cross 2 bacon slices, wrapping
bacon around potato. Bundle
wrap each potato (page 14).

Place on upper cooking rack.
Bake at MEDIUM with hood
closed until potatoes are
tender, 50 to 60 minutes.

4 servings

Au Gratin Potatoes

¼ cup all-purpose flour
½ teaspoon salt
⅛ teaspoon pepper
2 pkgs. (12 oz. each)
  frozen shredded hash
  brown potatoes, thawed
2 tablespoons chopped
  onion
1 cup shredded Cheddar
  cheese (about 4 oz.)
1½ cups half-and-half or
  milk

Preheat grill for 10 minutes.
Grease 1½-quart grill-safe
casserole. Set aside.

In large plastic food storage
bag, combine flour, salt and
pepper. Add potatoes. Shake to
coat. Place half of mixture in
prepared casserole. Sprinkle
with 1 tablespoon onion and ½
cup cheese. Layer with
remaining potato mixture, onion
and cheese. Pour half-and-half
over layers. Cover.

Bake using indirect MEDIUM
heat until potatoes are tender
and sauce thickens, 1 to 1¼
hours.

4 to 6 servings

Corned Beef and Cabbage ▲

1 large head cabbage
   (about 2 lbs.)
¼ lb. corned beef, thinly
   sliced

2 tablespoons beer
⅛ teaspoon pepper

Preheat grill for 10 minutes. Cut cabbage into 6 wedges, leaving wedges attached at base. Place on 24 × 18-inch double thickness of heavy-duty aluminum foil. Divide corned beef into 6 equal portions and place between wedges. Sprinkle cabbage with beer and pepper. Bundle wrap (page 14). Cook at MEDIUM with hood closed until cabbage is tender, 30 to 45 minutes.   *4 to 6 servings*

Baked Beans

3 slices bacon, chopped
⅓ cup chopped onion
2 cans (16 oz. each)
   great northern beans,
   rinsed and drained
1 can (8 oz.) tomato sauce

¼ cup molasses
2 tablespoons ketchup
1 teaspoon dry mustard
¼ teaspoon celery salt
⅛ teaspoon pepper

Remove cooking grid. Place 1½-quart grill-safe saucepan or dish directly on lava rock grate, arranging rocks around pan.* Combine bacon and onion in pan. Cook and stir at MEDIUM until bacon is light brown and onion is tender. Stir in remaining ingredients. Cover. Remove from heat.

Spread lava rocks evenly across grate with long-handled tongs. Replace cooking grid. Bake using indirect MEDIUM heat with hood closed until bubbly and flavors are blended, 30 to 35 minutes.

6 servings

*If your grill has two burners, cook over one burner only.

❶Oriental Vegetable Bundle

1 pkg. (10 oz.) frozen cut
   asparagus
1 can (8 oz.) sliced water
   chestnuts, drained
2 tablespoons teriyaki
   sauce
¼ teaspoon ground ginger
1 pkg. (6 oz.) frozen pea
   pods
1 ice cube

Preheat grill for 10 minutes. Place frozen asparagus* on 24 × 18-inch double thickness of heavy-duty aluminum foil. Arrange water chestnuts on top. In small bowl, mix teriyaki sauce and ginger. Sprinkle over vegetables. Top with frozen pea pods.* Add ice cube. Drugstore or bundle wrap (page 14).

Cook at MEDIUM with hood closed until vegetables are tender, about 20 minutes. Stir before serving.   *6 servings*

*Vegetables will thaw and break apart during grilling.

Rice Pilaf

1 cup white rice
½ cup broken vermicelli
⅓ cup slivered almonds
2 tablespoons butter or
   margarine
2 cups water
1 cup frozen green peas
¼ cup chopped onion
¼ cup diced carrot
1½ teaspoons instant
   chicken bouillon
   granules
½ teaspoon salt
½ teaspoon dried basil
   leaves

In 3-quart grill-safe casserole,
combine rice, vermicelli,
almonds and butter. Remove
cooking grid. Place casserole
directly on lava rock grate,
arranging rocks around dish.*
Cook and stir at MEDIUM with
hood open until vermicelli and
rice are light golden brown,
about 10 minutes.

Stir in remaining ingredients.
Cover. Reduce heat to LOW.
Cook with hood closed until
liquid is absorbed and rice is
tender, about 20 minutes.
6 servings

*If your grill has two burners,
cook over one burner only.

Marshmallow Yam Bake

4 medium yams, baked,
   opposite
½ cup applesauce
3 tablespoons butter or
   margarine, softened
1 tablespoon packed brown
   sugar
1 egg
¾ teaspoon salt
¼ teaspoon pumpkin pie spice
1 cup miniature
   marshmallows
⅓ cup chopped pecans

Preheat grill for 10 minutes.
Grease 1½-quart grill-safe
casserole. Set aside. Peel
baked yams and place in
medium mixing bowl. Mash
with fork. Add applesauce,
butter, brown sugar, egg, salt
and pumpkin pie spice. Stir until
smooth. Spread in prepared
casserole. Cover.

Bake using indirect MEDIUM
heat with hood closed, for 20
minutes. Uncover and sprinkle
with marshmallows and pecans.
Bake, uncovered, with hood
closed until marshmallows are
puffy and golden brown, about
5 minutes longer.   *6 to 8 servings*

●Greek-Style Zucchini

pictured on cover

4 small zucchini, thinly
   sliced*
1 medium tomato, seeded
   and chopped
¼ cup pitted black olives, cut
   in half lengthwise
2 tablespoons chopped green
   onion
1 tablespoon olive or
   vegetable oil
1 teaspoon lemon juice
¼ teaspoon dried oregano
   leaves
¼ teaspoon garlic salt
⅛ teaspoon pepper
   Grated Parmesan cheese
   (optional)

Preheat grill for 10 minutes.
In 1-quart grill-safe casserole,
combine zucchini, tomato, olives
and onion. In small dish, blend
oil, lemon juice, oregano, garlic
salt and pepper. Pour over
vegetables. Stir and cover.

Bake using indirect MEDIUM
heat with hood closed until
tender, 30 to 40 minutes.
Sprinkle with Parmesan cheese.
4 servings

*If desired, substitute 2 small
summer squash for 2 zucchini.

TIP: For a reduced-calorie
dish, substitute water for oil.

Foil-Wrapped Corn (4 ears)

Husk corn. Tear off 4 paper
towels. Cut 4 pieces of heavy-
duty aluminum foil, each slightly
larger than a paper towel.

Place 1 paper towel on each
piece of foil. Fold edges of foil
over towel. Pour ¼ cup water
onto each square.

Roll up corn inside foil square.
Fold ends under and press
edges to seal. Refer to chart
(opposite, for cooking time).

Vegetable Cooking Guide

ITEM	METHOD (Preheat grill for 10 minutes)	HEAT SETTING & COOKING TIME (with hood closed)
Acorn Squash, 2 1½ lbs. each 4 servings	Cut in half. Remove seeds. Combine ½ cup packed brown sugar, ¼ cup butter, 1 teaspoon ground cinnamon, ½ teaspoon pepper and ¼ teaspoon ground nutmeg. Place one-fourth mixture in each half. Bundle wrap* individually.	MEDIUM** 25 to 35 min.
🖤Asparagus 1 lb. 4 to 6 servings	Remove tough ends. Drugstore wrap* or place in covered casserole with 2 tablespoons butter and 2 ice cubes.	MEDIUM** 15 to 20 min.
🖤Carrots 1 to 1½ lbs. 4 to 6 servings	Cut into 2-inch pieces. Drugstore wrap* or place in covered casserole with 2 tablespoons butter, ½ teaspoon dried dill weed and 2 ice cubes.	MEDIUM** 20 to 25 min.
Cauliflower, whole 2 lbs. 4 to 6 servings	Trim outer leaves. Bundle wrap* with 4 ice cubes. After grilling, top with 1 slice of American process cheese and let stand, covered, for 2 minutes.	MEDIUM** 30 to 35 min.
Corn on the Cob 4 ears	Peel back husks but do not detach. Remove silks. Replace husks over ears. Use string to tie husks in place at end of each ear. Soak in cold water for 10 to 15 minutes.	MEDIUM** 20 to 25 min. (Turn 2 or 3 times.)
🖤Green Beans 1 lb. 4 to 6 servings	Remove ends. Drugstore wrap* or place in covered casserole with 2 tablespoons butter, ¼ cup slivered almonds and 4 ice cubes.	MEDIUM** 20 to 25 min.
🖤Mushrooms 8 oz. sliced or whole 3 or 4 servings	Drugstore wrap* or place in covered casserole with 1 tablespoon butter, 2 teaspoons red wine, dash pepper and dash salt.	MEDIUM** 8 to 10 min.
🖤Onions, 2 8 oz. each 4 servings	Peel and cut in half. Sprinkle with dash seasoned salt and dash fennel seed. Top each with 1 tablespoon butter. Bundle wrap* individually.	MEDIUM** 20 to 25 min. (Rearrange once.)
Potatoes, baked, 4 8 oz. each 4 servings	Lightly brush with vegetable oil, if desired. Prick several times with fork. Wrap each in single thickness of aluminum foil. Bake on upper cooking rack.	MEDIUM** 45 to 60 min. (Omit foil wrap for crisper potatoes.)
Potatoes, boiled 2 lbs. 4 to 6 servings	Peel potatoes. In grill-safe casserole, combine potatoes, 2 teaspoons salt and enough water to cover potatoes. Cover. Remove cooking grid. Place casserole directly on lava rock grate, arranging rocks around dish.**	HIGH until water boils, then LOW 15 to 20 min.
Yams, 4 8 to 12 oz. each 4 servings	Prick several times with fork. Wrap each in single thickness of aluminum foil. Bake on upper cooking rack.	MEDIUM** 45 to 60 min.

*See page 14.
**If your grill has two burners, cook and preheat over one burner only.
🖤 For a reduced-calorie dish, substitute water for butter.

Beverages & Appetizers

Why wait for the main course to use the gas grill? Welcome your guests with a grilled appetizer or hot beverage. Whether you're having a casual get-together or an elegant dinner, one of the recipes in this section will add a special touch. Grill Polynesian Kabobs on small wooden skewers. Serve Beer Cheese Soup in heavy mugs. Or offer Hot Fruit Punch in delicate glass cups. Let the gas grill get your party off to a terrific start.

◄ Hot Fruit Punch

> 1 jar (10 oz.) maraschino
>   cherries
> 4 cups water
> 4 cups apple cider
> 2 cups cranberry juice
>   cocktail
> 1 can (6 oz.) frozen orange
>   juice concentrate
> 1 can (6 oz.) frozen
>   lemonade concentrate

Drain maraschino cherries, reserving ½ cup juice. Set cherries aside. Place reserved juice in 3-quart grill-safe casserole. Stir in remaining ingredients except cherries. Remove cooking grid. Place casserole directly on lava rock grate, arranging rocks around dish.* Cook at HIGH with hood open until mixture is hot, 5 to 10 minutes, stirring occasionally. Garnish each serving with maraschino cherries.

8 to 10 servings

*If your grill has two burners, cook over one burner only.

Cinnamon Chicken Wings, page 82

Beer Cheese Soup▲

1 bottle (7 oz.) beer
⅓ cup water
1 teaspoon instant chicken
  bouillon granules
1 carrot, cut into 2-inch pieces
1 stalk celery, cut into
  2-inch pieces
1 small onion, quartered
1 bay leaf

6 whole peppercorns
3 tablespoons butter or
  margarine
3 tablespoons all-purpose
  flour
2 cups milk
1 jar (12 oz.) process cheese
  spread
  Popcorn (optional)

In 1-quart grill-safe saucepan, mix beer, water and bouillon granules.
In cheesecloth, tie carrot, celery, onion, bay leaf and peppercorns.
Add to beer mixture. Cover. Remove cooking grid. Place saucepan
directly on lava rock grate, arranging rocks around pan.* Cook at
HIGH with hood open until mixture boils. Reduce heat to LOW.
Simmer with hood closed until vegetables are tender, about 20 min-
utes. Discard vegetable bundle. Set broth aside.

Place butter in 2-quart grill-safe saucepan. Place pan on lava rock
grate, arranging rocks around pan.* Cook at MEDIUM until butter
melts. Stir in flour. Blend in milk. Cook and stir until thickened, 5
to 8 minutes. Reduce heat to LOW. Add broth. Stir in cheese
spread until melted. Garnish with popcorn.   *8 servings*

*If your grill has two burners, cook over one burner only.

Hot Spiced Cider

1½ quarts apple cider
  ⅓ cup packed brown sugar
  1 orange, sliced
  1 stick cinnamon
  1 teaspoon whole cloves
  1 teaspoon whole allspice
  ¼ teaspoon salt

In 3-quart grill-safe saucepan,
combine all ingredients. Remove
cooking grid. Place saucepan
directly on lava rock grate,
arranging rocks around pan.*
Cook at HIGH with hood open
until mixture boils. Cover.
Reduce heat to LOW. Simmer
for about 20 minutes.   *8 servings*

*If your grill has two burners,
cook over one burner only.

80

Polynesian Kabobs

1 lb. fresh sausage
   links, each link cut into
   3 pieces
1 can (8 oz.) whole water
   chestnuts, drained, or 1
   large green pepper, cut
   into 1-inch pieces
1 can (8 oz.) pineapple
   chunks, drained, (juice
   reserved)

Glaze:
2 tablespoons honey
1 tablespoon reserved
   pineapple juice
2 teaspoons soy sauce
⅛ teaspoon ground nutmeg
   Dash pepper

Soak twelve 6 to 8-inch wooden
skewers in water for 30 minutes.* Alternate sausage pieces,
water chestnuts and pineapple
chunks on skewers.

Preheat grill for 10 minutes. In
small bowl, mix all glaze ingredients. Grill kabobs at MEDIUM
with hood closed until sausage
is firm and light brown, 10 to
15 minutes, turning kabobs
over and brushing with glaze once.

12 appetizers

*Substitute metal skewers for
wooden skewers, if desired.

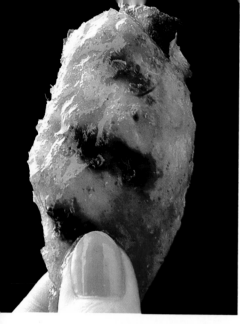

◄Cinnamon Chicken Wings

1 can (6 oz.) frozen
    pineapple juice
    concentrate, thawed
½ cup chili sauce
1½ teaspoons ground
    cinnamon

½ teaspoon chili powder
½ teaspoon onion salt
⅛ teaspoon cayenne
1 lb. chicken wings (8 or 9
    wings)

Follow photo directions below.

Cinnamon Ribs: Follow photo directions below, substituting 1½ lbs. pork spareribs, cut in half crosswise into sections 2 inches wide, for chicken wings. Marinate as directed. Season cooking grid with vegetable oil. Preheat grill for 5 minutes. Grill ribs at LOW with hood closed until tender, 25 to 30 minutes, turning ribs over and brushing with marinade once. Cut into individual pieces. *16 to 18 appetizers*

How to Make Cinnamon Chicken Wings

Blend all ingredients except chicken in small mixing bowl. Pour into glass baking dish or large plastic food storage bag.

Cut each chicken wing into 3 pieces at joints. Discard wing tip pieces. Place remaining pieces in marinade. Cover dish or close bag. Refrigerate for at least 8 hours, stirring or turning bag over occasionally.

Season cooking grid with vegetable oil. Preheat grill for 10 minutes.

Remove chicken wing pieces from marinade, reserving marinade. Grill chicken at MEDIUM with hood closed until meat near bone is no longer pink, 12 to 18 minutes, turning pieces over and brushing with marinade once.

Mini Quiches Lorraine ▶

⅔ cup butter or
  margarine, softened
4 oz. (half 8-oz. pkg.)
  cream cheese, softened
1⅔ cups all-purpose flour
1 cup finely-chopped
  fully-cooked ham
1 cup shredded Swiss
  cheese (about 4 oz.)
3 eggs
1 can (5⅓ oz.) evaporated
  milk
½ teaspoon salt
¼ teaspoon dried
  marjoram leaves
⅛ teaspoon pepper
6 slices bacon, cooked and
  crumbled

In medium mixing bowl, blend butter and cream cheese. Stir in flour. Shape into a ball. Wrap in plastic wrap and set aside.

In medium mixing bowl, blend remaining ingredients except bacon. Set aside.

Preheat grill for 10 minutes. Divide dough into 12 pieces. Place in 12 ungreased muffin cups. Press dough evenly in bottom and up sides of each cup. Bake using indirect MEDIUM heat with hood closed until light golden brown, about 10 minutes. Fill each pastry shell with a scant ¼ cup egg mixture. Top with crumbled bacon. Bake using indirect MEDIUM heat with hood closed until center is set and slightly puffed, 20 to 25 minutes, rotating pan once. *12 servings*

Frozen Appetizer Baking Guide

Frozen Pizza, Egg Rolls or Pizza Rolls	Preheat grill for 10 minutes. Place frozen item on baking sheet or large sheet of heavy-duty aluminum foil. Bake as directed on package, using indirect heat with hood closed. Use temperature guide on page 11 to determine correct heat setting. Place an oven thermometer on cooking grid over unlit burner. Regulate heat setting as needed.

Breads

Try something unique and delicious — bake bread in your gas grill! You can bake in your gas grill just as you do in a conventional oven. Prepare breads for a breakfast treat or as a complement to a grilled main dish.

The baking temperature of bread is important. The recipes on the following pages specify the heat setting and baking temperature that will give you the best results. Follow the directions on page 8 for using an oven thermometer in your gas grill. You'll get tasty grilled breads every time.

◄Pancakes

    1½ cups all-purpose flour
    1¼ cups milk
     ¼ cup powdered sugar
      1 egg, slightly beaten
      2 tablespoons vegetable oil
      1 teaspoon baking powder
     ½ teaspoon baking soda
     ½ teaspoon salt

In small mixing bowl, mix all ingredients. Stir until smooth.

Preheat grill for 5 minutes.* Season griddle with vegetable oil. Place on grid. Preheat for 5 minutes longer. Reduce heat to MEDIUM-HIGH. Pour ¼ cup batter onto griddle for each of 4 pancakes. Cook until surface is bubbly, 1½ to 2 minutes. Turn pancakes over. Cook until bottom is brown, 1½ to 2 minutes. Repeat with remaining batter.

Applesauce Pancakes: Follow recipe above, omitting powdered sugar. Decrease milk to 1 cup. Add ¾ cup applesauce and ¼ teaspoon pumpkin pie spice.   12 pancakes

*If your grill has two burners, preheat and cook over one burner only.

Cinnamon Monkey Bread

- 2 *pkgs. (¼ oz. each) active dry yeast*
- 1 *cup warm water (110° to 115°F)*
- 1 *cup shortening*
- 1 *cup boiling water*
- ¾ *cup sugar*
- 1½ *teaspoons salt*
- 2 *eggs*
- 7 *to 8 cups all-purpose flour*
- 1 *cup sugar*
- 4 *teaspoons ground cinnamon*
- 1 *cup butter or margarine, melted*

12 servings

How to Make Cinnamon Monkey Bread

Dissolve yeast in warm water. In large mixing bowl, combine shortening, boiling water, ¾ cup sugar and the salt. Beat at medium speed of mixer until shortening melts. Cool to 115°F.

Beat in yeast mixture and eggs. Mix in enough flour to form a stiff dough. Knead until dough is smooth and elastic, about 10 minutes, adding flour as needed.

Shape dough into ball. Place dough in lightly-greased large bowl. Turn dough over to grease both sides. Cover. Let rise in warm place until doubled, 45 to 60 minutes.

Grease 10-inch grill-safe tube pan. Set aside. Mix 1 cup sugar and the cinnamon in small bowl. Punch dough down. Divide and shape into 2-inch balls.

Dip each ball in melted butter. Roll in sugar mixture to coat. Layer in prepared pan. Cover. Let rise in warm place until doubled, 45 to 60 minutes. Preheat grill for 10 minutes.

Bake using indirect MEDIUM heat (350°F) with hood closed until bread is golden brown and sounds hollow when tapped, 45 to 60 minutes. Let stand for 10 minutes. Invert onto plate.

Cheesy Herb French Bread ▶

½ cup butter or margarine,
   melted
2 cloves garlic, minced
½ teaspoon dried basil leaves

1 loaf (1 lb.) French bread
5 slices Cheddar, Colby or
   mozzarella cheese (about
   ¾ oz. each)

Preheat grill for 5 minutes. In small mixing bowl, combine butter, garlic and basil. Set aside. Cut bread into 11 slices, leaving slices attached at bottom crust. Brush butter mixture on both sides of slices. Cut cheese slices in half diagonally. Place cheese triangles between bread slices. Drugstore wrap (page 14). Place bread on upper cooking rack. Grill at LOW with hood closed for 15 minutes.

Cheesy Herb Sourdough Bread: Follow recipe above, substituting 1 round loaf of sourdough bread for French bread. Cut into 11 wedges, leaving wedges attached at bottom crust. Continue as directed.

10 servings

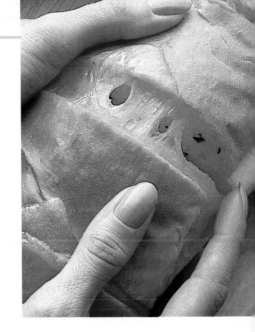

Orange Honey Rolls

pictured on cover

¼ cup packed brown sugar
¼ cup finely-chopped walnuts
2 tablespoons butter or
   margarine, melted
2 tablespoons honey
½ teaspoon grated orange
   peel

2 tablespoons granulated
   sugar
1 teaspoon ground cinnamon
1 loaf (14 oz.) frozen bread
   dough, thawed
2 tablespoons butter or
   margarine, melted
¼ cup finely-chopped walnuts

In 8-inch square grill-safe baking dish, mix brown sugar, ¼ cup walnuts, 2 tablespoons butter, the honey and orange peel. Spread evenly in bottom of dish. Set aside. In small bowl, mix granulated sugar and cinnamon. On floured surface, roll dough into 16 × 10-inch rectangle. Brush with 2 tablespoons butter. Sprinkle with sugar mixture and ¼ cup walnuts. Roll up, starting with longer side. Pinch edges to seal. Cut into 16 slices. Arrange cut-side down in prepared pan. Cover. Let rise in warm place until doubled, about 1 hour.

Preheat grill for 10 minutes. Bake using indirect MEDIUM heat (350°F) with hood closed until rolls are golden brown and sound hollow when tapped, 15 to 25 minutes, rotating pan once. Invert onto plate.

Onion Biscuits

1 can (2¾ oz.) French fried
   onions, slightly crushed
2 tablespoons butter or
   margarine, melted
1 teaspoon snipped fresh
   parsley
1 pkg. (10 oz.) refrigerated
   biscuits

Preheat grill for 10 minutes. In 8-inch round grill-safe pan, mix onions, butter and parsley. Spread in pan. Arrange biscuits on top. Bake using indirect MEDIUM-HIGH heat (375°F) with hood closed until biscuits are golden brown, 15 to 25 minutes. Invert onto plate.

Potato Biscuits: Follow recipe above, substituting 1 can (1¾ oz.) shoestring potatoes for French fried onions. *10 biscuits*

Frozen and Refrigerated Breads Baking Guide

Frozen Bread Dough	Defrost dough and let rise. Preheat grill for 10 minutes. Bake as directed on package, using indirect heat with hood closed. Use temperature guide on page 11 to determine correct heat setting.*
Frozen Muffins or Refrigerated Biscuits	Preheat grill for 10 minutes. Place muffins or biscuits on baking sheet. Bake as directed on package, using indirect heat with hood closed. Use temperature guide on page 11 to determine correct heat setting.*

*Place an oven thermometer on cooking grid over unlit burner. Regulate heat setting as needed.

Desserts

Serve a tasty grilled dessert as a delicious finish to a grilled meal. Your gas grill can be used to bake desserts like a conventional oven. This easy and unique way to bake is great for cookies, cakes, pies and more!

Perfect desserts depend on correct baking temperatures. The recipes in this section include both the heat setting and baking temperature that will work best. To determine the temperature inside your grill, place an oven thermometer on the cooking grid over the unlit side of the grill. When you bake, adjust the heat setting as needed to maintain the recommended baking temperature. Try our delicious recipes on the following pages. Or prepare your own favorite dessert on the grill, using the chart on page 11 to determine the correct heat setting.

◄Fudgy Coconut Pie

1½ cups sugar
¼ cup cocoa
2 eggs, slightly beaten
½ cup butter or margarine, melted
1 can (5⅓ oz.) evaporated milk
1 teaspoon vanilla
½ cup chopped pecans
½ cup flaked coconut
9-inch pie shell, unbaked
Frozen whipped dessert topping (optional)

In medium mixing bowl, combine sugar and cocoa. Add eggs, butter, evaporated milk and vanilla. Mix well. Fold in pecans and coconut. Pour into pie shell. Bake using indirect MEDIUM-LOW heat (325°F) with hood closed until center is set, about 55 minutes. Refrigerate for several hours. Serve with topping. *One 9-inch pie*

89

◄Fruit-Filled Pie

also pictured on cover

    Pastry for two-crust 9-inch pie
1 *can (21 oz.) fruit pie filling (any flavor)*

Preheat grill for 10 minutes.

Prepare pastry. Roll and fit bottom crust into 9-inch pie plate. Pour pie filling into crust. Top with upper crust or cut remaining pastry into ½-inch strips and weave across top to form lattice. Trim and flute edges. Bake using indirect MEDIUM heat (350°F) with hood closed until crust is golden brown and filling begins to bubble, 50 to 60 minutes.

One 9-inch pie

Applesauce Cake▲

2½ *cups all-purpose flour*
2 *teaspoons apple pie spice*
1½ *teaspoons baking soda*
1 *teaspoon salt*
1½ *cups granulated sugar*
½ *cup packed brown sugar*
⅔ *cup vegetable oil*
3 *eggs*
1 *teaspoon vanilla*
2 *cups applesauce*
½ *cup powdered sugar*
2 *teaspoons apple juice*

Grease and flour 12-cup grill-safe fluted ring pan. Set aside.

Preheat grill for 10 minutes. In medium mixing bowl, mix flour, apple pie spice, soda and salt. Set aside. In large mixing bowl, combine granulated sugar, brown sugar, oil, eggs and vanilla. Beat at medium speed of electric mixer until smooth, scraping bowl frequently. Add applesauce and flour mixture. Beat at medium speed of electric mixer until blended, scraping bowl constantly. Pour batter into prepared pan.

Bake using indirect MEDIUM heat (350°F) with hood closed until center springs back when touched lightly, 45 to 55 minutes. Invert onto serving plate. Cool. In small mixing bowl, blend powdered sugar and apple juice. Drizzle over cake.

One ring cake

Chocolate Chip Oatmeal Cookies

3/4 cup all-purpose flour
1 teaspoon ground cinnamon
1/2 teaspoon ground ginger
1/2 teaspoon ground allspice
1/4 teaspoon ground cloves
1/4 teaspoon baking soda
1/4 teaspoon salt
1/2 cup butter or margarine, softened
1/2 cup granulated sugar
1/2 cup packed brown sugar
1 egg, slightly beaten
1/2 teaspoon vanilla
1 1/2 cups quick-cooking rolled oats
1 pkg. (6 oz.) semi-sweet chocolate chips

In small mixing bowl, mix flour, cinnamon, ginger, allspice, cloves, soda and salt. Set aside.

In medium mixing bowl, cream butter, granulated sugar and brown sugar. Stir in egg and vanilla. Add flour mixture, mixing until smooth. Stir in oats and chocolate chips.

Preheat grill for 10 minutes. Drop dough by heaping teaspoonfuls about 2 inches apart on ungreased 12-inch round pan. Bake using indirect MEDIUM-HIGH heat (375°F) with hood closed until cookies are light golden brown, 12 to 14 minutes, rotating pan once. Cool slightly. Remove to wire rack.

2 dozen cookies

Brownies

1½ cups sugar
1 cup all-purpose flour
⅔ cup cocoa
1 cup butter or margarine,
    melted
3 eggs, slightly beaten
1 teaspoon vanilla
1 cup chopped nuts

Frosting:
1 cup powdered sugar
¼ cup cocoa
¼ cup butter or margarine,
    melted
2 tablespoons hot water

Grease and flour 9-inch square pan. Set aside.

Preheat grill for 10 minutes. In medium mixing bowl, stir together sugar, flour and cocoa. Add melted butter, eggs and vanilla. Mix well. Stir in chopped nuts. Pour into prepared pan. Bake using indirect MEDIUM heat (350°F) with hood closed until wooden pick inserted in center comes out clean, 45 to 60 minutes. Cool.

For frosting, in small mixing bowl, stir together powdered sugar and cocoa. Add melted butter and hot water. Stir until smooth. Spread on cooled brownies. Cut into 16 squares.   *16 brownies*

Dessert Mixes Baking Guide

Cakes, Cookies or Bars	Preheat grill for 10 minutes. Prepare batter according to recipe. Pour into prepared pan. Bake as directed on package, using indirect heat with hood closed. Use temperature guide on page 11 to determine correct heat setting. Place an oven thermometer on cooking grid over unlit burner. Regulate heat setting as needed.

Index